the Feminine Voice of Malta
il-Leħen Femminili ta' Malta

INTERNATIONAL HUMAN RIGHTS ART MOVEMENT

Curated & edited by Bridget Reaume

A publication of the International Human Rights Art Movement (IHRAM)

THE FEMININE VOICE OF MALTA
IL-LEĦEN FEMMINILI TA' MALTA

Copyright © 2024
International Human Rights Art Festival Inc., NY

All right reserved. No part of this publication may be reproduced, distributed, or transmitted in any form or by any means, including photocopying, recording, or other electronic or mechanical methods, without the prior written permission of the publisher, except in the case of brief quotations embodied in critical reviews and certain other noncompliance uses by copyright law.

For permission requests, contact Founding Producer Tom Block
and the IHRAM editorial team:
hello@humanrightsartmovement.org

Curated by IHRAM in the United States of America.
IHRAM, New York City, USA
www.humanrightsartmovement.org

Curator and Editor: Bridget Reaume
Proofreader: Lisa Zammit
Cover Design: Lisa Zammit
Cover Photo: Jahel Azzopardi
Featured on Cover: Francesca Vella

CONTENTS

Loranne Vella
Introduction 1

Maria Grech Ganado
Undefined 5

Anna Maria Schurmann
St Anthony, Please Come Around... 7
Something is Lost and Cannot Be Found

Miriam Calleja
Instruction Manual: Sheets of Desire 13

Elizabeth Grech
Musbieħ il-lejl | Firefly 15

Ramona Depares
Just A Game Of Football 17

Veronika Mercieca
Cassiopeia 25
The Letter Killeth but the Spirit Quickeneth 27

Lisa Zammit
Does it Beat This? 31

Aaron Aquilina
On Being Given a Photo My Mother Did Not Want 33
Baby at the Abortion Rally 35

Claudia Gauci
Farka ikħal | A Grain of Blue 37

Clare Azzopardi
Konfessjonijiet qabel norqdu | Before We Sleep 49

Anna Grima
Marija is-sewda 58

Jahel Azzopardi
The Weight of Their Silence 60

Veronica Veen
Għonnella: Divergent Views 62

Brenda Prato
Il-Kumdità tas-soċjetà | The Amenity of Society 67

Leanne Ellul
Il-ġrajja ta' Marjanna (mill-ġdid) | 71
The tale of Marjanna (once more)

Loranne vella
Immacolata Concetta (Marta Marta Excerpt) 83

Louis Briffa
Tale of a Grasshopper and a Tomato | 99
L-istorja ta' gurat u ta' tadama

Kristina Borg
Wombs on Strike 107

Nadia Mifsud
il-plural ta' jiena mhux dejjem aħna | 111
The Plural of I is Not Always We

Rita Saliba
Vjola bħax-xaħxieħ 117

Lara Calleja
Tixtieq ittir | Would You Like to Fly? 119

Fiona Mallia
To Live With Hope 121

INTRODUCTION

LORANNE VELLA

THIS VOICE IS OUR WEAPON.

We, the voices in these pages, have witnessed our mothers, grandmothers, daughters, sisters, ourselves, being systematically cornered into silent submission, obedience. Into becoming servile, weak, passive, absent and invisible. Into giving up our dreams to become loyal wives, diligent homemakers and caring mothers. Into giving up our right to our own thoughts, to our aspirations, to our very own body. By our own fathers, uncles, brothers, husbands; by the strict teacher, the pious priest, the arrogant policeman, the ethical doctor, the righteous judge; by tradition, religion, the law, the state. Our body is labeled female, weak, from birth and a life is chosen for us. We are expected to live it passively, quietly, obediently. A tremor finds a way into our hushed voices: we soon learn that our words will be deemed spineless while they are still forming as thoughts. We lack presence, we lack validity. We teach ourselves to be very afraid. Some have been killed for daring to speak out.

This anthology brings together several writers that have often, especially in previous decades, been grouped together—by a corpus of male writers, critics and academics who looked at us curiously, condescendingly but also warily—under the somewhat derogatory subheading "Malta's women writers", that is, a category apart. For many years, seeing the label of "female writer" for what it was—a mark of difference, a label assigned to us to keep us in our place because our writing does not really count—I refused to be referred to as "a female writer". "I am a writer," I used to rebut, "just a writer, like any other writer, irrespective of our gender." Until it occurred to me that writing from a female perspective is actually a very powerful political stance. This is writing from the very core of this woman's body aiming at not only subverting and perverting the aesthetic and cultural ideals dictated by the literary hegemony, but truly dismantling abuse and oppression in all their forms and at all levels. It is, I finally understood, not our weakness that threatens— how can weakness be a threat?—but our strength, our fierceness, our anger, forever played down by those in authority as incoherence, madness or hysteria. No wonder we've been kept apart, quiet and at a distance. Our voices are our weapon against the patriarchy which in Malta has always manifested itself in the form of the domineering single voice of the Catholic priest, the lawyer or head of state (almost always male), and the father as head of the nuclear family.

In the words of one of the characters in my novel *Marta Marta*, when one puts on the glasses of feminism, one becomes more aware of, and attuned to, other forms of oppression by the strong over the weak. And it is very often the case that the oppressor is one and the same—the patriarchal and capitalistic mentality that stands for and promotes heteronormativity, whereby the binary of male and female (and where male is strong and active while female is weak and passive, to name but a few binary traits attributed to these two) is the only possible and acceptable idea of normality. So, at a time when we're witnessing new forms of gender oppression, it is important to make it clear that feminist writing is concerned with the struggles of those (women, trans, non-binary) who find themselves in the intersection of different forms of oppression. Our stories may be altogether different, but what we have in common is the abuse we suffer because of who we are. These voices are very often silenced because they might sound out of tune, in discord with the dominant heteronormative (usually white, but definitely always patriarchal) culture.

The works in the following pages are a testimony to the fact that in every story there is someone—whose reality is perhaps different to ours—who is struggling to make their voice heard. They deserve to tell their story, they deserve our attention. With our work we declare: they/we shall not remain silent anymore. For they/we have a story to tell, a history to rewrite, and a new future to bring about.

Loranne Vella
Author, Translator, Performer
Malta
June 2024

The Voices

✺

L-ilħna

UNDEFINED

MARIA GRECH GANADO

She was a body framed by creation to bear its future,
sometimes its sins, often its censure:
guilty of opposing definitions not her own

betraying grammar with imprecisions that defied hold
defied his stories
defied his God trapped in a pronoun.

She is a woman undefined now, of herself made –
her language relaxes in a new embrace
without his possessive case.

I was born in 1943 and wrote 'UNDEFINED' at the age of 80 because, even in 2024, I consider Malta's society still predominantly patriarchal. The Constitution of Malta establishes Catholicism as the state religion and, since the 2021 census of the population found that 82.6% belonged to the Catholic church. I believe this is still reflected by elements of the island's culture even now, especially its hierarchy of male authority and the prejudices this engenders.

The initial title of the submitted poem was 'Possessive Case' because of the implications of the masculine pronoun, but I decided to stress the freedom of a woman's essence instead. In fact, much of my earlier feminist poetry is a battle cry of protest from the dominant conviction that women were specifically created for the orthodox role of a wife and mother.

NITOLBOK SANT'ANTNIN...
SIB IL-ĦWEJJEĠ MITLUFIN

"ST ANTHONY, PLEASE COME AROUND...
SOMETHING IS LOST AND CANNOT BE FOUND"

ANNA MARIA SCHURMANN

"NOW, WHERE DOES this go?" said my Mum holding the long yellow bread knife, my Dad's prized possession.

I lifted my gaze from reading the paper on the kitchen table, smiling. I was home in Malta enjoying the European summer escaping the cold Melbourne winter. I had just eaten way too many slices of "ħobż biż-żejt" — my dad's famous sandwiches — crusty sourdough bread spread with fresh tomatoes, olive oil, capers, goat cheese, and Mediterranean herbs picked from our garden.

Having spent the majority of her life running the family home, my mother Carmen seemed to derive a particular joy from making fun of my dad's habits and quirks.

"Ha ha ha," I flattered my mum, "I wonder where its storage place is…"

My mum stared back at me blankly, no hint of humour in her kind, hardened face, and repeated her question: "Where does this go?"

I realised, to my horror, that she was not joking — my mum was actually wondering where the bread knife goes. My mum was losing her marbles.

Everyone knew the story of the yellow breadknife. It was a gift from Kevin, my brother Albert's friend, a chef. Often at our house, Kevin had witnessed my dad slicing loaves of bread and making fresh sandwiches for all his six kids and their friends for hours on end.

My dad loved it. I am not sure if it was the ease with which the bread knife sliced through the fresh bread or whether it was the fact that for once someone had looked him in the eye and said — "I see you. I know hard you have worked all your life. This is for you."

The bread knife was a prized possession, never to be placed in the dishwasher, wiped with its own special cloth, blade neatly tucked into its transparent plastic holder. It was placed on a special shelf on top of a special hand towel, away from the curious hands of the growing number of grandchildren.

Since I had flown in, I reiterated to my five siblings that something was not right with our mother. I could not put my finger on it but something was just... off.

"She's just growing old", they laughed me off.

"She's always been forgetful."

"That's just because you don't see her daily like we do."

That much was true. Having lived overseas for more than 10 years, I certainly did not see my mum and the rest of my family on a daily basis. I did however speak to her very often.

Growing up, my mum's episodes of forgetfulness were a source of immense entertainment for us all. We made fun of how many phones and reading glasses she lost and how she hid treats and gifts so we could not pounce on them, only to forget where she hid them.

There was a familiar pattern — first she would declare with confidence that whatever she had misplaced would inevitably just turn up. "Perhaps if you kids were a bit tidier, things would be easier to find." she would fire. Then, slowly, the confidence would begin to wane and she'd start lamenting how forgetful she was becoming. Finally, and this was absolutely the last resort, she would call upon the intervention of Saint Anthony of Padua, the patron saint of lost things.

"Dear Saint Anthony, please come around: something is lost, and it cannot be found," she would repeat a few times.

"If you always placed things in the same spot or returned them from where you took them, you would not need Saint Anthony," my dad would note as he sat at his desk where there was not one staple or paper clip out of place.

"He'll help me," she would say. "He always does."

Sure enough, once the misplaced objects were located, Saint Anthony would always take credit. In the event that said object, such as her wedding ring, was never found, Saint Anthony appeared to be absolved of all responsibility, my mum's confidence in his abilities seemingly intact. My siblings and I would jokingly note that surely a wedding ring (of a Catholic marriage union that produced several offspring) should have been given top priority on Saint Anthony's list and that he had manifestly underdelivered this time round. All to no avail. Saint Anthony ruled supreme as my mum's favourite saint, a fact she reminded us of every year on 13 June — the feast day of Saint Anthony of Padua.

"What do you mean where does the bread knife go?" I finally told my mum, who was still looking at me questioningly, as if it was the first time she had seen it.

"Mum, it goes where it has always been stored," I said as I gently took the knife out of her hand and put it in its place.

"Of course," she said swinging back into normal conversation as if nothing had happened. "I forgot."

That evening, I took my dad to the side. "What is going on?" I said, relating the bread knife incident.

My dad lowered his glance, sadness spreading all over his face. "You haven't seen anything yet."

And one by one, my dad started listing a spate of incidents, one more worrying than the other. The previous week, my mum had gone for a local shop, and got completely lost. A neighbour had found her walking around confused and walked her home. Pots had been left on the stove, with many dinners burnt. Just the previous day, she had put a load of washing on and forgotten to put the laundry in.

13 June 2017

Back in my parents' house for another European Summer break, I can hear my dad coming in through the front door. I am still in bed but he has already been out to the baker's before the heat sets in to get my favourite bread. I strategically time my entry into the kitchen as he proudly brings out the loaf and starts making his famous sandwiches.

"Do you want one?" he smiles.

"If you insist," I smile back.

Then I see the sadness creeping back in his face again: "Mum won't be able to come with you to the bridal shop today. She's just not up to it."

I looked at him, incredulous. I had specifically decided to get married in Malta so that my Maltese family and especially my mum would be fully part of it. All our lives, my mum, my sister and I had spoken about how we would go to bridal shops together, trying dresses on.

My mum, the person who loved fashion, the person who sewed her own wedding dress, and made endless outfits for us did not feel like coming to a wedding shop to see her daughter try on her wedding dress. If I ever needed a sign that my mother was no longer herself, it was right there, on a plate.

In truth, the signs were everywhere — the first signs of neglect in the house that was usually cleaned spotlessly in anticipation of my return, the unfiltered comments she never used to let slip and the endless hours spent in bed.

"You just *have* to mum", I said as I literally dragged her out of bed, into the shower, and forced her to join me, thinking of all the times she had ordered me to get out of the bed and not waste the day.

"Thank you for pushing me to come," she said later, "I really enjoyed that. You looked beautiful. I do not know who I am anymore." As I hugged her, I tried to hide my tears. Within my embrace, I could hear her quiet sobbing.

※

13 June 2023

I am back home in Malta following a COVID-imposed absence of three years. I try to quicken my pace but my four-year old daughter insists on inspecting every aspect of this unfamiliar landscape wondering why elderly people are sitting outside their homes engaged in lively chatter with their neighbours. In the pram, my eight month old smiles at everyone and everything that comes our way.

"Mr and Mrs Bonnici?" asks the receptionist at the aged care home, teetering on her high heels. "Room 424," she says — you must be the daughter residing in Australia."

"Sure am," I say, adjusting my mask and waving my COVID-19 vaccination certificate.

Since my last visit, the string of 'forgetfulness' incidents had started to pile up, making it impossible for my dad, ten years older than my mum, to manage. My dad, who had hardly ever changed a baby's nappy in his lifetime, suddenly had a wife who needed the attention of a newborn. My dad, who had never cooked a meal in his life, had cornered my sister one evening to take notes on how to make my mum's signature *brodu* (chicken broth). From then onwards, he cooked that broth almost every night.

Then came the night when my mum wet the bed. In the end, he could not cope — he begged us to find them a spot in a nursing home where they could be together. In an instant, they moved from our family home of five bedrooms and a big garden full of citrus trees, to one room in a nursing home. Within a couple of months, as a pandemic unexpectedly took over the world, they were prevented from leaving that one room for fear of catching a virus that could kill them while they slowly died inside.

As I walk into the tiny room overlooking the ocean, my dad gets off his seat and rushes forward to hug me. He has aged and looks so old. Over his shoulders, I get the first glimpse of my mum and my heart sinks. She's sitting in a wheelchair, hands clenched in an unnatural fist — she does not budge. I bend down and look into her eyes — those sparkly blue eyes we all wanted to inherit but only my sister did. She stares at me, a blank look — as if she's trying to will her brain to place me.

"Who am I?" I say, after a few minutes.

She continues to stare at me and I start wondering if I have also aged beyond recognition.

"You are my daughter!" she finally says. From the corner of my eye, I can see my dad gently smile. "That's more than I expected", he says gently almost inaudibly.

"She can't remember my name," I tell him almost begging him to tell me she eventually will.

"It's more than I expected," he repeats.

"And who are these kids?" she suddenly says, glancing at my daughters. "I did not know you had any children."

I glance back at my dad, the familiar sadness once more clouding his face. "Of course you know who they are," he tells her as he shows her the pictures and cards I had sent on her bedside table.

"What day is it today?" my four-year-old suddenly asks, still struggling to make sense of life in a different continent and fighting jet lag.

"Today is the feast of St. Anthony", her granddad says.

"Dear St. Anthony, please come around: something is lost, and it cannot be found…" I mumble. *"Nitolbok Sant'Antnin… sib il-ħwejjeġ mitlufin."*

> *This story is about coming to terms with a mother's illness, particularly when you live on the other side of the world and as you start navigating motherhood yourself.*

INSTRUCTION MANUAL: SHEETS OF DESIRE

MIRIAM CALLEJA

i. The problem - Look what you made me do

she's had / is / too much / has / vodka tonic / had / a short skirt / hiked up / spiked / who'd you look at? / she's got that / look / doesn't order salads / eats / like a man / too many phone numbers saved / open plan / who sits beside you? / where have you been? / the past is / we both know what that means / de—col—le—tage / why would you wear / perfume / why would you need / when you have me / look what you made me do / erase the past / delete / tame / your laugh / pictures / you asked for it call my bluff / look / it won't happen again / if you / quit / don't text / bad / mad woman / hysterical girl / enough / why do you look at / slut / you don't know what's good for you / quiet / the neighbours will hear / don't cry / I'll buy you another / one too many / here here / the last time / you are mine / nobody will love you like I do / look what you made me do / look what you made me do / look what you made me do.

ii. The solution - Instruction manual

1. Align Desire (diagram 1) with Lack of Desire (diagram 2) so that the seams touch. You may notice a difference in size, as shown in the image on the box. *Note: contents may have shifted during transportation.*

2. Leave 1" overlap on the window of the face. Clean the face's surface, ensuring it is free from oils, lotions, tears, and dust.

3. Sprinkle tears on both the face and the sheets of desire. The first set of tears has been provided. Kindly go to the company website if you cannot provide your own.

4. Starting from the top, apply gentle pressure while squeezing the air out in brisk, firm strokes. Do not change your mind.

5. Use the fourth finger to soothe the face. Ensure the eyes are covered well by dissolving true-lust in them. Imitation lust will not produce a long-lasting effect.

6. The nose must be stuffed with whims warmed up in a bain marie.

7. Speak your last true words before applying the sheets over the mouth; remember to bite on the word NO before letting it dissolve under the tongue. Wait for the fizz to start before completely closing the sheet over the chin.

*In case of a severe allergic reaction, please panic and scream to liberate yourself within a few minutes.
**Warnings: I am not a toy, only a woman to toy with.

> *This poem is divided into two parts to elucidate the traps of domestic violence and the consequences of expecting women to fit a norm. I aim to show the socialised fears of women who live in societies that they believe would not protect them if they needed to escape dangerous spaces or circumstances.*

MUSBIEĦ IL-LEJL

ELIZABETH GRECH

Kun af
li dakinhar li sawtitni
l-qilla ta' kliemek,
frixt sħaba griża
fuq ruħi,
ċarrattli ħsibijieti,
benġiltli ġildti saff saff
kissirtli s-sinsla ta' dahri
rukkell wara rukkell.
Imma,
ara taħseb,
ruħi musbieħ il-lejl
inemnem
sakemm
ġismi midbul
jerġa' jqum
fuq sħaba
bajda
mifruxa.

FIREFLY

ELIZABETH GRECH
TRANSLATED BY IRENE MANGION

Let it be known
that the day the wrath of your words
came crushing down on me,
a grey cloud unfurled
on my soul
rupturing my thoughts,
bruising layer upon layer of skin
shattering my backbone
one disk at a time.

But harbour no illusions:
like a firefly
my soul
will flicker
until my broken body
rises again
on a long stretch
of cotton-white cloud.

I believe poetry needs not be explained. It is felt, echoing in the heart and mind. Like this poem, whose words hurt the body and soul with intentional blows. It encourages the reader to recollect their fragments and fully take their power back again. Let no one and nothing break your soul.

JUST A GAME OF FOOTBALL

RAMONA DEPARES

YOU START LIFE with stars in your eyes, cocooned in frilly dresses, princess tiaras, and shiny, pink ballerina shoes. You decide that this is perfection, a world of sunshine that you've done nothing to deserve.

Until you try to trade your shiny, pink ballerinas for sturdy running shoes, so you can kick a ball on the streets with your brother. You ask your mother's permission, and her face speaks thunder.

"*Binti*, you don't want people thinking you're a tomboy. Here, let's go knit a wedding dress for your Barbie, that's way more fun."

Your eight-year-old brain doesn't get it, confident she'll change her mind when you ask her again the next day. She doesn't. Your mother, whose face usually speaks love and softness, now speaks a mood you don't understand.

You only start to get it when you try to sneak out with your brother to play with the other village boys, and you're marched back indoors to help with dinner. You can't believe you hadn't spotted this before. One set of rules for boys, and another - much more limiting - set for girls.

The unfairness of it all takes your breath away and you start shrieking right there, on the door-step.

"*Binti*, you're not a boy. You're a young lady, so behave like one. I'll show you how to make those roast potatoes you love."

It's just a game of football, you think. Who cares?

But you do care. And, over the years, football becomes curfew time, your hemline, the stash of condoms confiscated by your father even as your brother parades a succession of girls through the front door in the early hours of the morning. Football is when you're asked to use a softer tone when speaking to your father and brother, and to stop being so damn argumentative because no-one likes bossy, sarcastic girls anyway.

Football.

Freedom.

Boys have both.

You have neither. Becuase you're a young lady.

Aged 14 you get your first period and life comes with a new and bewildering set of rules. Always cross your legs when seated. Don't be too friendly with the boys, or you'll give them the wrong idea.

No-one needs to see you walk to the bathroom tampon in hand, that's just gross. And whatever you do, don't get a stain on your skirt or your life is over.

It takes you four weeks to understand that this is no exaggeration as you waddle to the bathroom, while the kids at the church youth centre you're forced to attend for fun twice a week howl and whistle. The priest who's on chaperoning duties throws you dirty looks and the words in his eyes sting. Gross. Tainted. Stupid.

The following week, one of the boys who bayed loudest asks you out. You're confused. But he's cute, so you say yes. You go on a hike past the Red Tower in Mellieħa, where - using a degree of pressure that would have an older woman running for the hills - he persuades you to have sex. You're not quite sure what's going on, because sex education at your catholic school was limited to the nun's quick and mumbled, "the sperm meets the egg, and conception takes place."

How does the sperm meet the egg, you ask. The nun's reply leaves you even more perplexed.

"It just does."

So you're there, your bare butt on the prickly gorse while this boy enthusiastically pierces your very being, and ohmigod that hurts. You clench up so badly that your stomach starts cramping and you ask him to stop, but he keeps pushing anyway and you can't breathe and you think if you just lie still it'll soon be over.

And it is, and everything's okay after all. It's the same year that champion bowler Sylvia King is kidnapped by two men and burnt alive in Kunċizzjoni. Other women have bigger problems than you.

On the way back home the boy shares his Mars bar with you and chats about the parish disco party that's coming up on Saturday, as though he didn't just have you pinned to the ground, your whimpered 'stop' fizzling out unacknowledged.

Years go by and the pain and shame of unwanted sex grow numb. You never use the word 'rape', even to yourself. That would be ridiculous. You did lie there, after all.

You read about Vanessa Grech, who is cut up with a penknife and left to rot in a well by the man who wants to keep his affair secret. He does the same to Vanessa's 17-month-old baby Ailey. You thank the stars above that you've been lucky enough to avoid such men.

You're excited about your new job with a magazine, even though so far it's more about making toasties than breaking stories. You're there, buttering and jamming with the enthusiasm of someone young enough for cholesterol to be a far off myth, when one of the sales execs sidles up from behind and pinches your ass.

You want to skewer his filthy hand with the knife but, instead, you laugh nervously.

"Good ass," he says playfully, helping himself to half of your toast.

You hate yourself for not making a fuss, and you stop going to the office kitchen by yourself. It's 2002, and Pauline Tanti has just been shot dead by her estranged husband. A month later, Rachel Muscat is stabbed to death by the boyfriend she's trying to break up with. She's 20 years old.

A few years fly past, and you've put the kitchen grope behind you. You even use it as an amusing anecdote at parties sometimes, as though to say, "Ha! I was so stupid back then, I'd totally chop off his balls if anyone tried to pull that crap on me today."

You're lying. You're now a grown woman and you still avoid situations where you're alone with a male colleague at the office. You carry a rape whistle everywhere you go and, when walking the dog after dark, you hold your house keys firmly in hand in the ridiculous belief that if someone were to attack you you'd be able to pull some bold move and floor them.

And you've blocked the numbers of a score of delivery men on your phone. Those same men who, the very next day after delivering your loot, slide into your WhatsApps with a, "Hey dear, still alone? Want some company?"

You don't want to make a fuss. The headlines of the day are focused on Lourdes Agius, who is found strangled in her own home. Her partner is let off on a plea of insanity.

A new delivery brings a new unsolicited message. But you'd feel stupid reporting this, it seems too trivial. So whenever you open the door to a strange man you take to shouting out random terms of endearment to your imaginary husband, waiting in your non-imaginary kitchen.

"Babe, get the food on the table, I'll just be a second," you chirp out cheerfully. A part of you is disappointed when your imaginary husband fails to reply, but at least the random WhatsApps stop.

Until suddenly your imaginary husband is imaginary no more and you're over the moon, dazzled with orgasms and actual home-cooked dinners and hey, maybe being a woman is not so bad after all.

And then, one evening, he decides that the skirt you're wearing makes you look "thrashy." It doesn't, even Sister Dolores from the fake sex ed classes wouldn't have bat an eyelid. You refuse to change, so he refuses to come to your colleague's birthday party with you. And he refuses to speak to you for a week until, one day, you wake up and he's reaching for your breasts like nothing happened.

You freeze, but it would just be too weird to stop him and the constant silent treatment is getting to you. And so you let it happen, without protest, in the hope it doesn't happen again.

It happens again with predictable regularity. Every time you have plans to go out, in fact, and you kind of get used to the toxic silence and just start ignoring the whole thing. Until one day he changes the rules of the game.

"You're not going out like that."

And he pushes you in the bedroom and locks you there until the morning, when he opens the door bearing coffee like nothing happened. You walk out of the house straight to the police station. You pack your bags and beg your mother to take you in, temporarily. You don't afford to rent another place and you need all your money for a good lawyer to get him kicked out of the apartment you paid for.

"*Binti*, did he beat you?"

"No, ma."

"Can't you just not wear tight clothes? Are you sure you want this?"

He makes things difficult, of course, so it takes more than a year of court mandated counselling to get him out of your apartment and to get your life back. Finally, it's back to imaginary husbands and bad dates. And sex that you're not quite into, but that you go along with because it's easier than making a fuss and risking aggro.

COVID hits and your anxiety is spiralling. Not because of the virus, but because a few weeks before it all started you had one of those let's-get-it-over-with sessions and now you're three weeks late and all the airports have just closed.

You used protection but, well... we all know an 'oops the condom broke' baby or two. You can't afford a pregnancy, much less an actual baby. Mentally, or financially. Before this, you never quite appreciated your privilege of being able to hop on a short flight to the UK or to Italy. What did other women do before Ryanair and easyJet, you wonder.

You start researching the possibility of getting abortion pills posted directly until, thank fuck. Your panties are stained bright red. You start breathing again.

The whole thing shakes you. Even after the pandemic is done, you stop dating. No more agreeing to sex out of politeness. It's never just a game of football.

It takes time, but you get better at being you. You don't automatically stop talking when your male colleague interrupts your presentation. You don't block WhatsApp numbers from strangers. You tell the strangers to fuck off and to stop messaging you or you'll file a harassment report.

Then, poor Paulina Dembska is strangled and raped, bang on the Sliema promenade, by a young man who doesn't even know her. But the devil made him do it. You join a 100 other Maltese women in a vigil to help raise awareness about femicide. You stop feeling obliged to be polite to the rando who interrupts the conversation with your girlfriends at the bar. And you're ready to use the pepper spray you got off ebay if things start looking even vaguely dicey.

You stop keeping your tummy tucked in Every. Single. Minute. Of. The. Day.

It takes time, but you start feeling comfortable in your own skin. You cultivate friendships with like-minded women and, slowly, the pressure of years of molding yourself to the expected shape starts easing.

You become extremely selective, and you have no qualms walking out of a handful of bad dates. You see more women around you slowly trying to shrug off years of indoctrination, of being told how they should behave and what they should look like. You start thinking that there's hope for today's generation of young, starry-eyed women, after all.

Until Bernice Cassar is shot by her estranged husband right on a busy main road in Paola and no-one does anything to stop it. *It's never just a game of football.*

JUST A GAME OF FOOTBALL

RAMONA DEPARES | AUTHOR REFLECTION

I live in a country where women who campaign for reproductive rights are publicly assaulted on the streets. Where a husband who beats up his wife is released on bail, so he can go back home and rape her. Where a woman with mental health issues is dragged to court by her abusive partner for trying to have an abortion — and a substantial portion of the country supports the arrest.

I wrote Just A Game Of Football in the hope it inspires other Maltese women to actively be part of the fight for full gender rights by simply saying 'no' to even the smallest actions that threaten equality.

Just A Game Of Football documents the typical life of an 'average' Maltese woman through a composite of anecdotes. Some of these are my own personal experiences. Others were shared with me during interviews and research sessions that I conducted with a number of Maltese women. Compared to the institutionalised gender violence we see reported globally, these experiences may not be the most shocking. But they are endemic to my home country, and widespread enough to continue cementing the unequal footing of women in Maltese society.

I am grateful that I don't live in a part of the world where the majority of us are raped, beaten or murdered. But this does not mean that we enjoy a life of freedom and equality. Until we start fighting to remove even the most apparently inconsequential of discriminatory acts, the bigger picture is likely to remain unchanged.

CASSIOPEIA

VERONIKA MERCIECA

NINSTAB F'WIĊĊ L-ILMA taħt il-ħarsa ta' Cassiopeia. Is-sema rifless f'għajnejja huwa bħal borma mtaqqba u mdawwra għal fuq rasha. Madwari hemm il-baħar iswed mejjet u mill-bogħod jinstemgħa l-għajjat taċ-ċief minn ma' wiċċ l-irdum. Il-bikja tagħhom tirbombja mal-ħitan ġganteski u toħloq kor infernuż li jilħaq 'il-widnejja moħbija taħt l-ilma. Minn dejjem stħajjilt din il-bikja kerha ma' dik ta' tarbija li tilfet lil ommha.

Ninstab qalb dan il-baħar skur u kalm, imdawra bl-irdum u issa se nagħlaq għajnejja. Widnejja jisimgħu l-mewġ igorr u nimmaġina l-irdumijiet jiżfnu u jduruni, jagħlquni u jifgawni. F'dan il-mument nixtieq li l-mewġ jiblagħni.

Nintelaq kompletament, idejja u saqajja taħt l-ilma, filwaqt li żaqqi, rasi u l-bqijja ta' ġismi jibqgħu jmissu mal-arja. Arja sħuna t'Awissu li tifgak iktar mill-ilma mielaħ tal-baħar.

Hawnekk ninstab mitlufa u waħdi. Taħti hemm baħħ iswed li donnu qed jixrob id-dawl tal-istillel. Qalbi qed inħossha ankra li ser tnizzilni magħha fil-fond tal-baħar. Min jaf jekk meta ninstab hemm taħt inkunx nista xorta nilmħek, Cassiopeia?

O Cassiopeia, int li minn dejjem kont fl-isfond ta' ħajti, illum qiegħda nħoss in-niket tiegħek. Illum għandi uġigħ kbir f'qalbi li jista' jimla sax-xifer il-borma tas-sema tiegħek. Ngħid jien li dan l-uġigħ jfur anki mit-toqob tagħha u jinżel bħala xita lura għal fuqi. Ngħarraq id-dinja kollha bid-dmugħ u niket filwaqt li nibqa' mdendla f'wiċċ l-ilma baħar żejtni. Donnu kilt xi mħar irrabjat imneħħi minn postu b'sikkina li taqta' għax f'ħalqi hemm togħma morra.

Cassiopeia, m'iniex se nitolbok biex tgħinni iżda nixtieqek tismagħni meta naqsam qalbi miegħek. Int li emmint li sbuħitek hija l-aqwa fid-dinja. Int li offendejt poteri akbar minnek u li minħabba hekk ġejt ikkastigata u sfurzata mid-destin biex teżilja ruħek qalb is-silenzju tas-smewwiet. Ismagħni u arani issa, kif qiegħda ngħum bejn il-blat aħrax ta' madwari.

Ma' min nista' naqsam dak li għandi ngħid, ħlief mal-ħarsa tal-vanità eterna? Ifhimni Cassiopeia, għax bħalek jien ukoll sħitt lili nnifsi bit-twemmin tiegħi.

> 'Cassiopeia', captures an episode of personal disappointment and frustration. It is the moment I realised that I was in an unhealthy relationship which would soon reach its end. At the time, I felt isolated and detached from my feelings and I found it difficult to open up to anyone about what I had been going through. Swimming at night beneath the dark cliffs of Xlendi, I floated and looked up to the stars, turning towards the familiar constellation and figure after which the piece is named. Dealing with feelings of shame, pride and vanity, I felt myself reflected in Cassiopeia's story of hubris and exile. As the haunting cries of the shearwater echoed down the rugged cliff walls, I surrendered to my imagination and allowed myself to share with them my painful moment of realisation. I also draw upon different references, including the classical understanding of the night sky as an inverted colander, as well as the 'sour' experience of eating a sea urchin. Writing a rough copy of the work shortly after getting back onto the shore, I found in my hands this lament which conveys a plea for understanding inspired by natural and mythological elements.
>
> This is the only piece of writing I have written entirely in Maltese in the past 5 years and it is also the only piece of writing which I believe, would lose significant meaning if it were to be translated into English. I would like to thank the author Leanne Ellul for her careful consideration of this work and Maria Giuliana Fenech for instilling in me an appreciation and love for the classics.

THE LETTER KILLETH BUT THE SPIRIT QUICKENETH

VERONIKA MERCIECA

A SMALL FRUIT FLY landed on the page and distracted me. I smothered it reflexively under the imperial force of my finger and continued reading Mr. Merton's words on God. He spoke in riddles and I exerted myself in trying to decipher their meaning. It was useless though as my eyes kept drifting to the blood-stained page against which the bug was crushed.

Right by the trail of insect innards were the following words *to place your trust in visible things is to live in despair.*

I mused on these words for a while and my thoughts went to where the author never intended them to lead.

I was transported to a day earlier on in summer. The warm air blew from the sea up the northwestern hills of Żebbuġ into a restaurant terrace where I was sitting with my mother waiting for pizza. We were on holiday and had decided to have a night out to ourselves. Knowing from a young age that she will some day lose her eyesight, my mother always made an effort to pick the most beautiful places for food and rest. This day was no exception.

We were sat on the edge of the terrace and the sun was setting below us. Yellow burnt hills rolled down into the blue sea which, in the heat, turned white at the horizon and merged with the sky. It was as though the scene was painted in one singular brushstroke.

There was an issue however, as the terrace was filled with huge beetles that were flying around in a bizarre way. They hit the walls, chairs and table en masse and some were already lying dead nearby. Occasionally, some people let out startled grunts as the beetles hit their arms or legs.

As I began discussing this strange business with my mom, one hit our table and fell over backwards. The poor thing seemed to be weighed down by its own body. Its legs outstretched, it rocked in its attempts to turn over.

Seeing this pitiful sight, we decided to try and help this poor creature who had been participating in the unexplainable frenzy. My mom took out a sheet of paper that she had folded in her bag and handed it over to me. I got up from my chair and squatted down next to it, placed the paper beneath its wings and turned it back onto its legs. Before we could watch it crawl or fly away however, the beetles intensified their assault and a man who was sitting at a table nearby stood up loudly, his chair scraping against the ground. Hearing the noise, I turned and watched as he stepped on every beetle there was, including ours.

Once his massacre had ended, he turned to us with a smile, as though to say 'problem solved'. I sat down and felt slightly sick. He had clearly assumed that we were trying to move the beetle away from us and he probably thought that he had done all the restaurant goers a great favour by putting an end to these unexpected and unpleasant-to-most projectiles.

My mother sighed and looked back out over the railings and into the sea. I turned my gaze at the remains of the beetle we had intended on helping.

Were its legs still moving?

I watched these futile attempts for a time without thinking, unconsciously waiting for him to resume his flight, as one waits for a machine that has stopped momentarily, to start again without considering the reason for its failure.

Would it still be alive had we remained in our place?

A few months prior, I had read Virgina Woolf's *The Death of the Moth*. She had called the insect 'a tiny bead of pure life' which, through its movements, displayed the true nature of life.

This insect's legs had, however, stopped moving.

Aristotle, as I had later found out, named the beetle κολεόπτερος in his attempts at natural categorisation. This classification, a combination of κολεός (sheath) and πτερόν (wings), struck me in the aftermath of this outcome, as highly ironic and tragic. The shielded warriors had gone for a siege but they left their swords at home.

THE LETTER KILLETH BUT THE SPIRIT QUICKENETH

VERONIKA MERCIECA | AUTHOR REFLECTION

The Letter Killeth but the Spirit Quickeneth, *is a reflective essay responding to a biblical quotation by way of an experience I had in Gozo. As with many other families in Malta, mine would often head to our sister island in the summer for a few moments of leisure, silence and respite. In an episode of beetle frenzy and a failed rescue at a restaurant, I join the authors Thomas Merton and Virginia Woolf in musing on themes of empathy, misunderstanding and the ironies of existence.*

DOES IT BEAT THIS?

LISA ZAMMIT

As I stand at a red light, I get
visions of an old warmth in my bones —

> *il-mama*, eyes firmly closed and fingers dancing with
> the rosary beads, her rhythmic Ave Maria's filling the
> comfortable silence.

> *in-nannu* and I sitting on the seaside's edge, legs dangling
> in the rough waters, surrendering to the
> wave's slapping games.

> the strong aromatic smell of *iz-zalza ħamra* drifting
> from my childhood kitchen, as I sit below the sun's rays,
> meaty thighs peacefully exposed and book in hand.

I fight against the harsh Scottish winds, the sky depressingly dull.
I remember why I ran away, but I now think
*does it beat this? This feeling of loneliness, unfamiliarity,
homesickness for a home that is no longer?*

I left behind the claustrophobic streets, a loud language,
a culture blinded by its own ignorance, and a people
brainwashing you into their false expectations:

> "You should calm down or you'll never find a boyfriend like that."
> "Cover your belly because you don't want to show that to people."
> "No children or religion? Don't be a fool, you'll change your mind —
> you're too young to decide."

Was it all worth it? you ask.
Well, time will tell, *ħbieb tiegħi*.

The ocean where I learned to swim and became a lover of the sea—that represented adventure and new beginning—was also a 219km coastal barrier, confining us to the same people, same traditions, and same generational experiences on a loop. Growing up in Malta was both wonderful and limiting.

We are a blend of flavours, cultures, and languages, making up a uniquely beautiful people and culture. But there are three things that Maltese people will kneel to and hide behind: tradition, religion and politics — they whisper underneath our society like gossip; always generating new lies, polluting people's lives, and powering the corrupt.

Traditionally, women left work after the birth of their first child, devoting their life to acting as housewives, whether they liked it or not. Girls were told that in order to attract a boy they would need to look after their figure and maintain a feminine attitude. Doctors would blame a woman's ailment on her high BMI, ignoring her claims of pain during sex because she's deemed clinically overweight, according to the male-generated data. Brothers were given more freedom on nights out, whereas girls were told to come home hours before. If an old man's eyes wandered across your body hungrily one day, you were questioned on your attire and if you were acting provocatively. If you got openly angry one day at how your society was treating women and girls, you were told to shut up and sit quietly, like a precious doll.

This anthology explores themes of gender stereotypes, rape, rigid expectations, abuse, abortion, and being a woman in a Catholic country. Every Maltese woman has experienced something different, but every voice, leħen, *is meant to be heard, loud and clear.*

ON BEING GIVEN A PHOTO MY MOTHER DID NOT WANT

AARON AQUILINA

Father, who looked and walked and grew a beard just as I would –
he the originator, I the facsimile –
holding my older sister, then barely three, saying to the camera *I think
she is as delicate as she smells, a powdered Turkish Delight*

>All this before he became himself, cutting us deep:
>the shards of glass door shrapnelling
>when he smashed it in my sister's face.

Sister, who burrows into herself, a mourner of dead love –
she wears a veil, heirlooms the family's trauma in a wooden box –
in those rare occasions of siblingiarity tells me *People still
look at the scars on my wrist and get the wrong idea*

>But I walk away from her words, walking
>her father's footsteps. I do not want
>the wooden box she might bequeath me.

Father, only real in photographs, his most recent clothes
bought in the 'nineties, sometimes makes the plaintive call
that comes through my phone: *Happy Christmas*, some years
You didn't even text me on my birthday (or other holidays, events).

>What I am supposed to say to the man
>who almost killed my sister and then again
>again several times over, I don't know…

I can look once more at the photo.

A short reflection stemming from personal experience of domestic violence, through which I attempt to navigate my own position — as a man — in relation to the women in my life, despite me being very similar, in some ways, to their aggressor (my father). My mother, who experienced the worst of it, is in the poem likewise constrained to just the title: a position of "headship" that offers no voice, strength, or real visibility. My sister's pain, and my avoidance of it, is given some voice, but my father's haunting of us takes up the most space.

BABY AT THE ABORTION RALLY

AARON AQUILINA

I

Walking through the capital, a sleek suit's stomping ground. The turnout is middling. Some of us, who cannot engender but via the surrogacy of biblical history or the robotic friction of science fiction, want the rain to wash the shop fronts

and water the pips of grass peeking between cobblestones. A chant begins, a stomping-back, and we are clapping at Burger King, strudel stands, ATMs, statues of knights, the courthouse, past a glowing Guess which asks no questions.

II

This is my view: you, my friend, who made me promise you over morning
                                       pills
Yes I will take you up to Sicily for an abortion, no questions asked, our secret
holding the hand of a dyke, strands of hair coloured in defiance neon. Some other queer

folk cross the crossed streets (crosses watch from church doors, memories too); women march, sidestepping puddles, burning steps against the rising tide of those leaving work, driving imported cars away from imported thoughts. My eyes rest on

a woman, scarf over hair, teeth through smile, pram driven with the reckless caution of experience. A baby sleeps there, blankets keeping warm the plastic base of a flag flapping BODY, CHOICE — its pronouns lost in the folds — its sleep unperturbed by our drummed visibility. The baby: maybe the first Ouroboros, protesting its own birth, speaking up between one soft breath-bubble and another: saying: proclaiming: something I do not quite hear, because two priests pass by with bent heads, their murmurs deafening.

III

People descend from the stage, having been illegal for more than two hours now. The crowd begins to find its way apart. With nothing in hand except soggy cardboard, I move to move, but subtly follow you, pram-god, pram-prophecy: wanting is not everything.

A recollection of my thoughts during a pro-choice rally I attended. The poem makes my (and others') position of queerness visible — I am queer, and it is queer that I am there, since this is not a problem I will ever myself go through or fully understand. I view the rally as one of those pivotal moments of tension between global progressive thought and insular conservative feelings, as well as navigating the issues of the personal and the collective. I try to make these clashes visible in the poem. The fact that a woman in support of abortion rights brought her baby with her is, to me, powerfully emblematic, but in ways that cannot be fully articulated lest they fall back into dogmatic thought.

A GRAIN OF BLUE

CLAUDIA GAUCI

ENGLISH TRANSLATION OF "FARKA IKĦAL" TRANSLATED BY ALBERT GATT

SHE HAD STARTED to live only for those few hours in the morning, which were hers alone. Getting into the van, she'd pick up a newspaper, drive down to the shore and go to the usual cafe. At her favourite table facing away from the cafe, she would open the paper, order a cappuccino, light a cigarette and let the sea sink into her eyes. She'd stare at it for a long time, it made her shiver and she'd feel herself restored a little more.

As usual, her paper remained unread, her coffee practically untouched, while her cigarette smouldered on the edge of the ashtray, its half-spilled guts crumbling in the breeze. There was nothing else she needed to do. Every day she left her sewing room behind littered with tacked fabric, a heap of dresses like discarded skins abandoned on the table under a neon light (which she had probably forgotten to turn off this morning, as usual). She left behind her shape and her husband's in the crushed bedsheets, a space wide enough for two between them. She left behind the greasy dishes in the sink and an overflowing garbage can in the backyard. The radio was still on, tuned in to the usual frequency where she could catch her favourite programme, the one that played a lot of songs by Elton John. Her children would get up and go to work and she wouldn't see them off. With everyone gone she was left alone, chewing on her thoughts and her worries about this house that had changed so completely, where silence had spread over the walls like mould.

He'll be here soon. Usually, he turned up at around ten. Tight jeans, black leather jacket and a cigarette between his fingers. Today she'll ask him to delete the picture he took of her yesterday on his phone. She was taken aback when she saw her own placid face dappled with sunlight filling the small screen. She hadn't realised he was taking it. And he just showed it to her and said nothing, as usual. Just smiled and held up his phone so she could see. She doesn't know why she keeps coming here, at the same table and at the same time. She doesn't know why, before going out in the morning, she's started to enjoy rummaging through her boxes of earrings and putting on those nice ones, the brightly coloured ones that suited her so much when they dangled from her ears. She doesn't know why she's gone back to wearing v-neck sweaters, especially the two blue ones whose colour was an echo of her eyes. She'd given up on those two in particular since the operation, but now she's discovered that they're not that revealing; in fact, she looks a little better with a slightly plunging neckline, rather than the grip of a turtleneck.

He's been meeting her every day for two weeks now. He knows she owns a white van, that she lives in Żabbar, that she's married and has kids and he knows, too, that she doesn't talk so much and prefers to look out over the sea rather than at him. But he hasn't given up. Several times he's caught her looking at him out of the corner of her eye.

"Ma, are you going out again today?"

"Yes. I'll be off soon."

"Did the little one wash her hair yesterday? Tell her to wash it because it was reeking to high heaven."

"Yes, she's washed it. It was a mess this morning when she left, though, 'cause I overslept. The honking from the school bus woke me up. At least she was up and dressed already."

"Haven't you talked to papa yet, ma?"

"There's nothing left to say, is there? He's owned up to it and won't be going there again. But that doesn't mean much. He doesn't act normal with me anymore. Can't you see what he's like? All clammed up! Never wants to go anywhere! I can't bear talking to him anymore. Every time I speak to him it feels like I'm dying. I wish I'd passed away during the surgery. I don't think I can remember how to smile anymore."

"Will you shut it, ma. Don't talk like that! It's probably just a phase, it'll pass."

"I don't know. I'm going to hang up. I'm off."

"Bye ma. See you tomorrow. I'll be staying the night at Joseph's."

"All right. Take care now. Bye."

As soon as she hung up she went to the bathroom, checked that her mascara hadn't run, put some perfume on, took the keys to the van and left.

In that house, the days had begun to pile up like bones in a mass grave. Next month it'll be twenty-eight years since they got married. Twenty-eight years of peeking out from framed pictures dotted all over the house. She'd always felt they were happy — they had a family, the occasional holiday, the garden she had always wanted.

And then the illness came.

Her husband had already started going abroad for work but after her surgery he'd arranged to stay in Malta for longer, at least until the worst was over. When she saw herself in the mirror the first time after months of therapy, her world was turned upside down. Her skin was grey, the colour of the bathroom tiles. Her head was bare, except for a few hairs at the back. She felt sick. Her arms, her legs, her belly had gone flabby and felt heavy. The only colour left was that grain of blue in her eyes. That week they went to get her fitted with a wig, and somehow she began to come back to the land of the living.

Her grandfather was mad, or so her mother said. He had once drawn a huge cross in the backyard with the blood from a rabbit he'd slaughtered and made his daughters swear that they'd never fall pregnant by some depraved young man. He swore he'd cut the throat of the first among his children who brought dishonour upon his name. She can feel it, her grandfather's madness, it's running through her veins. She's started to feel it spreading through her brain and crushing her every time she hears the dull ringtone of her husband's phone. Or when she glimpses the screen lighting up in the dark when she can't go to sleep. She never picked up the phone. She knew that if she looked down, the words would fly up like a cloud of mosquitos, cling to her skin and suck every drop of her blood.

So she would lie in bed, tossing and turning, mulling things over in the sodden sheets as the pillows grew heavy with her pain. Like a band around her head, that streak of madness would tighten and twist and wouldn't let up until she went downstairs to the kitchen, eyes open wide, and she opened the drawer and took out the biggest knife and brought it down with all her strength on her arm, letting the colour of blood and bruising bleed against the white cupboards while her husband rushed downstairs, the veins throbbing against his temples. His lips a thin, white line.

He was late that morning. She sat at the table outside as usual, the cappuccino still untouched before her, her cigarette gasping its last breath and the pages of the newspaper turning on their own in the breeze. She'd been there for about two hours, with the taste of the sea on her tongue, reclining comfortably in her chair. That day she felt at one with the chair she sat on, with the warm, constant sun, with the rocks and the sea a stone's throw away. Time had stopped to wait for her.

At last he turned up. Out of the corner of her eye, she saw him striding towards her table, confident as ever. The closer he got, the more fixedly she stared out at the sea, her neck going stiff, her heart beating violently and her eyes smarting because she wouldn't allow herself to blink. He sat down beside her, ordered a black coffee and waited, sometimes looking around, sometimes at her. The coffee arrived and he gulped it down. She was still looking at the sea but now a smile played on her lips. He looked at her without moving. They kept this up for a bit, listening to the nervous slap of the water against the rocks. Suddenly he stood up, took his wallet out of his trouser pocket, rummaged for some change, dumped the coins on the table and stood there, his head bowed towards her, his eyes searching for hers.

She didn't move. Her neck had gone numb. She felt his questioning glance come down on her head like freezing rain. How much longer before he made his move? What would he do? Slowly, she tilted her head up and caught his gaze. She stood up then, grabbed her handbag and pushed her chair back against the table. He turned his back to her and started walking and she followed. They came out onto the sun-drenched street, crossed to the other side, walked past her van and turned the corner. She felt relieved to find herself in the shade. The street was narrow and it was deserted. He walked on until he reached the last of the three cars parked along there, occasionally glancing back at her with a brief smile. He opened the door on his side and got in behind the wheel, slammed his seat back, reached over to the passenger side and opened the door so she could get in beside him. She kept her eyes fixed on the ground as she got in and sat down beside him and once there all she could do was stare at the dashboard, clutching the small handbag in her lap, pressing it against her stomach, her earrings swinging without a sound.

'You're so beautiful, do you know that?'

She said nothing. She leaned in against him with a sideways glance. He put his arms around her promptly. Holding her tight against him he kissed her hair and her cheeks and her lips. She yielded to his embrace and let him do as he pleased without responding. His hands roamed along her thighs and rose along her back and neck, found their way beneath her sweater and pulled it up. He stopped. His eyes, which he'd kept shut all this time, opened slowly. His hands were on her breasts. Slowly he removed them and his eyes lingered on her incongruity. One side was smooth, full, white, healthy; the other was hollowed out, livid and empty. She just looked at him. The tears welled up. Their breathing was more shallow now and everything was still except for the screech of a cicada outside in the sun.

He pulled her blouse down slowly, wiped the tears from her cheeks and kissed her. Starting up the car, he drove her back to her van. She got out of the car, took the keys from her handbag, opened the door and got into the van. Behind the steering wheel, she continued to look at him as he drove slowly away and disappeared round the corner.

She sat there a while longer. Today, she had parked right on the shoreline. Below her was the sea. If she swung her legs away from her seat, her feet would immediately find the rocks. Two steps and she'd be in the lap of the sea. No one else was there. She got out of the van, locked it and started walking down along the rocks until she got to the edge. Taking off her sandals, she paddled her feet in the water. It felt cold, a blade slicing through her flesh. She smiled. She stood up and walked further. The rocks weren't too slippery and the sea was so clear she could easily find her footing. She took a few more steps until the water reached her thighs and her skirt was clinging to her sides. The chill of the water was making her gasp. She kept on smiling. She waded further out until the water rose to her chest. She didn't mind the chill anymore. She could stand there for a long time.

The sky above and the sea below, rocking her in an endless blue. The weight she had felt only a short time before seemed to be rising through her head, leaving her empty and weightless. She couldn't stop smiling. She walked on. The water was now up to her neck. Her earrings came away and floated on the surface beside her and their colours mingled with the sea and it swelled in a gentle embrace.

This short story follows a nameless woman dealing with the aftermath of breast cancer surgery. Her body is not what it once was. Through her eyes, she is monstrous and yet she is trying to resurface through the trauma and scars the cancer left behind. The experience left her family shattered, particularly her relationship with her husband, who is distant, cold, and possibly unfaithful.

A new stranger enters her life and finds her beautiful, reigniting a passion within her. The stranger makes her feel desirable again, prompting her to act on her instincts despite her guilt. The ending is ambiguous, leaving her fate open to interpretation: does she find renewal or succumb to despair?

Inspired by a real woman who faced similar struggles, this narrative highlights the profound impact of cancer on personal and family dynamics, and the fleeting solace found in unexpected connections.

FARKA IKĦAL

CLAUDIA GAUCI

ORIGINAL MALTESE VERSION OF "A GRAIN OF BLUE"

SARET TGĦIX GĦAL dawk il-ftit sigħat filgħodu li kienu tagħha biss. Taqbad il-vann, tmur tixtri l-gazzetta, tasal sax-xatt u tmur fil-kafetterija tas-soltu. Tpoġġi fuq il-mejda li tħobb hi, daharha lejn il-ħanut, tiftaħ il-gazzetta, tordna kapuċċino, tqabbad sigarett u tħalli l-baħar jitrekken f'għajnejha. Tħobb tħares lejh fit-tul u hu jtiha dehxa lura li tfejjaqha ftit ieħor.

Bħas-soltu, il-gazzetta ma taqrahiex, il-kafé bilkemm tmissu u s-sigarett tħallih imqabbad fuq xifer l-ash tray, imsarnu nofshom barra jitfarrku fiż-żiffa. Mill-bqija ma jkollha xejn x'tagħmel iktar. Kuljum tħalli warajha kamra tal-ħjata mimlija tixlil, gozz ilbiesi skarnati, tagħha u tat-tfal, mitluqa fuq il-mejda bid-dawl tan-neon (li aktarx dalgħodu reġgħet insiet titfi) jagħti fuqhom. Ħalliet il-forom tagħha u ta' żewġha bi spazju ta' mill-inqas żewġ persuni bejniethom, mgħaffġin mal-lożor. Ħalliet il-platti mdellka fis-sink u ż-żibel imfawwar fil-bitħa. Ir-radju baqa' jagħti, dejjem fuq l-istess frekwenza ħalli tinżerta l-programm favorit li jdoqq ħafna diski ta' Elton John. Uliedha jqumu u jitilqu għax-xogħol mingħajr ma tarahom biex issellmilhom. Meta jitlaq kulħadd tibqa' hi weħedha, tomgħod il-ħsibijiet u l-inkwiet tagħhom dwar din id-dar li nbidlet għal kollox, fejn is-skiet tela' sew mal-ħitan bħal moffa.

Dalwaqt jiġi issa. Is-soltu xil-għaxra jitfaċċa. Ġins issikkat, ġakketta sewda tal-ġilda u sigarett bejn subgħajh. Illum se ssaqsih biex iħassar dak ir-ritratt li ħadilha lbieraħ bil-mowbajl. Inħasdet kif rat wiċċha kwiet bid-daqqiet rotob tax-xemx fuqu jimla l-iskrin żgħir. Qas kienet indunat li ħadu. Meta urihulha ma qal xejn, kif kien iħobb jagħmel hu. Kemm tbissem u tella' l-mowbajl 'il fuq biex tarah. Ma tafx għaliex baqgħet tmur hemm xorta, fuq l-istess mejda u fl-istess ħin. Ma tafx għaliex, qabel toħroġ filgħodu, qed tieħu gost tqalleb fil-kaxex tal-imsielet u terġa' tilbes dawk l-ikkuluriti, tħosshom sbieħ jitbandlu jagħjtu ma' widnejha. Ma tafx għaliex reġgħet qed tilbes flokkijiet bil-v-neck, speċjalment dawk it-tnejn blu li kienu l-eku ta' għajnejha. Kienet qatgħethom dawk speċjalment minn wara l-operazzjoni imma issa qed tinduna li tassew

43

ma kien jidher xejn, anzi kienet tidher aħjar b'dik id-daqsxejn skullatura milli bl-għenuq tondi jitremblu ma' għonqha.

Issa ilu xi ħmistax dan jiġi ħdejha kuljum. Jaf li għandha vann abjad żgħir, jaf li toqgħod Ħaż-Żabbar, jaf li hi miżżewġa u għandha t-tfal u jaf li hi ta' ftit kliem u tippreferi toqgħod tħares lejn il-baħar milli lejh. Imma ma qatax qalbu. Qabadha tħares lejh minn taħt il-għajn kemm-il darba.

'Ma, erġajt ħierġa llum?'

'Ijwa. Daqt isir il-ħin.'

'Ħaslitu xagħarha lbieraħ iż-żgħira? Għidtilha biex taħslu għax kien jinten seba' pesti.'

'Iva, ħaslitu. Dalgħodu telqet bih imgerfex imma, għax bqajt rieqda jien. Il-ħorn tal-vann qajjimni. Anzi kienet diġà qamet u libset.'

'Għadek ma kellimtux lill-papà, ma?'

'Xi tridni ngħidlu aktar? Ammetta issa u mhux se jerġa' jmur. Imma ma jfisser xejn. M'għadux l-istess miegħi. M'intix tarah kif sar? Bla kliem? Qatt ma jkun irid joħroġ! Ma niflaħx inkellmu iktar. Inħossni qed immut kull darba li nipprova nkellmu. Aħjar ħadni Alla fl-operazzjoni. Inħossni lanqas għadni naf nitbissem'

'Aqtagħh'istja ma. Titkellimx hekk! Abbli din faży kerha, issa tgħaddi.'

'Ma nafx. Ħa naqta' ta. Ħa mmur.'

'Ċaw ma. Narak għada. Illejla se norqod għand Joseph.'

'Owkej. Oqgħdu attenti ta. Ċaw.'

Kif qatgħet marret fil-kamra tal-banju biex tara ċallsitx il-maskara, għamlet ftit fwieħa, qabdet iċ-ċwievet tal-vann u telqet.

F'dik id-dar, il-ġranet bdew jinġemgħu gozz fuq xulxin qishom għadam ġo foss komuni. Xahar ieħor jagħlqu tmienja u għoxrin sena miżżewġin. Tmienja u għoxrin sena jittawlu minn ġol-frejms tar-ritratti mxerrdin mad-dar kollha. Dejjem ħasset li kienu kuntenti – bil-familja li kellhom, b'xi safra kultant, bil-ġnien li dejjem xtaqet. Imbagħad tfaċċat il-marda. Żewġha kien diġà beda jmur barra fuq xogħol iżda wara li operawha kien irranġa li jibqa' Malta għallinqas sakemm tgħaddi l-burraxka. Meta ħarset fil-mera għall-ewwel darba wara xhur ta' terapija d-dinja nqalbet ta' taħt fuq. Laħamha, bħall-madum griż tal-kamra tal-banju. Rasha għerja, ħlief għal ftit xagħar fuq wara. Telagħlha l-istonku. Dirgħajha, riġlejha u żaqqha mpaħpħin u tqal. L-uniku lewn kien l-ikħal f'għajnejha. Dik il-ġimgħa marru jixtru parrokka u b'xi mod reġgħet lura fid-dinja tal-ħajjin.

Nannuha, skont ommha, kien miġnun. Fil-bitħa kien għamel salib kbir b'demm il-fenek li qatel u ġiegħel lil uliedu bniet jaħilfu li qatt mhuma se jinqabdu tqal minn xi ġuvni xxellerat. U hu ħalfilhom lura li jekk xi ħadd minnhom iwaqqagħlu ġieħu kien lest iħanxarlu għonqu. Dak il-ġenn ta' nannuha issa qed tħossu jiġri fil-vini tagħha. Saret tħossu jikber ġo moħħha u jgħaffiġha kull darba li tisma' l-mowbajl ta' żewġha jdoqq dawk iż-żewġ noti mqanżħa. Jew fid-dlam, meta ma tkunx tista' torqod tilmaħ l-iskrin żgħir jixgħel bla ħoss. Ma kinitx taqbad il-mowbajl f'idha. Kienet taf li jekk tħares ġo fih il-kliem itir għaliha bħan-nemus, jaqbad ma' laħamha u jerdagħlha demmha kollu. Kienet tibqa' fis-sodda titqalleb u thewden bla ħsejjes, il-lożor għasra, l-imħaded tqal bl-ugigħ. Dik iż-żigarella ġenn ġo moħħha taqbad tissikka u tistira u ma terħix qabel ma tinżel isfel fil-kċina b'għajnejha mberrqin, tiftaħ il-kexxun tas-skieken, taqbad l-ikbar waħda u tniżżilha bis-saħħa fuq driegħha sakemm il-kuluri tad-demm u t-tbenġil jitħalltu fuq il-kabords bojod u żewġha jinżel jiġri, il-vini ta' nagħsu mqabbżin xiber 'il barra. Ħalqu linja rqiqa bajda.

Dik l-għodwa kien iddawwar. Bħas-soltu kienet mal-mejda fuq barra, bil-kapuċċino quddiemha għadu mimli sa fuq, bis-sigarett iħarħar l-aħħar nifsijiet tiegħu u l-gazzetta tqalleb il-folji weħedha fiż-żiffa. Kienet ilha hemm xi sagħtejn, ittiegħem il-baħar, mitluqa telqa ħelwa fuq is-siġġu. Dakinhar kienet qed tħossha ssir parti mis-siġġu, parti mix-xemx fietla u konsistenti, parti mill-blat u l-baħar tefgħa ta' ġebla 'l bogħod. Iż-żmien kien waqaf jistennieha. Fl-aħħar tfaċċa. Minn taħt il-għajn ratu miexi lejn il-mejda tagħha bil-mixja soda u kunfidenti tiegħu u iktar ma joqrob lejha iktar bdiet tiċċassa lejn il-baħar,

45

għonqha jibbies, qalbha tħabbat bil-goff u għajnejha jaħarquha għax ma ridtix itteptiphom. Intasab ħdejha, ordna kafé iswed u qagħad jistenna, daqqa jħares madwaru u daqqa lejha. Il-kafé wasal u xorbu f'nifs. Hi kienet għadha qed tħares lejn il-baħar imma issa kellha tbissima żgħira. Qagħad iħares lejha bla ma ċċaqlaq. Baqgħu hekk għal ftit tal-ħin, jisimgħu l-mewġ żgħir iħabbat nervuż mal-blat. Ħin minnhom qam bilwieqfa, ħareġ il-kartiera mill-but tal-qalziet, gerfex għaż-żgħar, tefa' l-muniti fuq il-mejda u baqa' wieqaf, rasu baxxuta 'l isfel fid-direzzjoni tagħha, għajnejh ifittxuha. Hi ma tniffsitx. Għonqha ma baqgħetx tħossu iżjed. Il-mistoqsija f'għajnejh ħassitha nieżla fuq rasha bħal xita ffriżata. Kemm se jdum ma jiċċaqlaq? X'se tagħmel? Bil-mod dawret rasha 'il fuq u laqgħet il-ħarsa tiegħu. Qamet hi wkoll, ħafnet il-handbag f'idha u ressqet is-siġġu mal-mejda. Hu dar daħru lejha u qabad miexi u hi bdiet miexja warajh. Ħarġu fit-triq maħsula bix-xemx, qasmu għan-naħa l-oħra, għaddew minn ħdejn il-vann tagħha u kisru mal-kantuniera. Ħadet ir-ruħ kif sabet id-dell. It-triq kienet żgħira u dejqa u ma kien hemm ħadd. Baqa' miexi lejn l-aħħar mit-tliet karozzi pparkjati, kultant iħares lura lejha u jitbissimlha ħafif. Fetaħ il-bieba tan-naħa tiegħu u daħal wara l-istering, ressaq is-sit tiegħu lura b'tisbita, iġġebbed lejn il-bieba l-oħra u fetħilha biex tidħol tpoġġi ħdejh. Għajnejha kienu qed iħarsu lejn l-art hi u dieħla biex tpoġġi magenbu u xħin intasbet hemm baqgħet tiċċassa lejn id-dashboard, il-handbag żgħir magħfus ma' żaqqha, l-imsielet twal jitbandlu bla ħoss.

'Int taf kemm int sabiħa?'

Ma tkellmet xejn. Ħarset lejh minn taħt u inklinat ftit lejh. Hu kien pront laqagħha u dawwar driegħu magħha. Għafasha miegħu u bisilha xagħarha u wiċċha u xofftejha. Kif rat hekk intelqet iktar f'dirgħajh u ħallietu jagħmel li jrid bla ma kompliet miegħu. Idejh ġrew ma' koxxtejha u telgħu għal daharha u għonqha, daħlu taħt il-flokk u għollew 'il fuq. Waqaf. Għajnejh li kienu magħluqin infetħu bil-mod. Idejh kienu magħluqa ma' sidirha. Neħħiehom bil-mod u ħarstu baqgħet titnikker fuq sidirha stunat. Naħa mimli, lixx, abjad u b'saħħtu, naħa mħaffer, misluħ, vojt. Hi baqgħet tħares lejh. Id-dmugħ lest biex jaqa'. In-nifsijiet tagħhom kienu battew għal kollox u issa kien hemm ħemda kbira ħlief għall-werżieq jagħjat fix-xemx barra.

Niżlilha l-flokk bil-mod, mesħilha d-dmugħ minn ma' wiċċha u biesha.

Startja l-karozza u ħadha ħdejn il-vann tagħha. Hi ħarġet minn ġol-karozza, ħarġet iċ-ċwievet tal-vann minn ġol-handbag, fetħitu u telgħet fih. Baqgħet tħares lejh minn wara l-istering sakemm telaq bil-mod minn ħdejha u għeb wara l-kantuniera. Baqgħet hemm għal ftit ħin ieħor. Il-vann kienet ipparkjatu max-xatt eżatt illum. Taħtha kien hemm il-baħar. Tniżżel riġlejha minn fuq is-sit u kienu jmissu mal-blat mill-ewwel. Żewġ passi u tkun f'ħoġru. Ma kien hemm ħadd. Niżlet mill-vann, sakkritu u qabdet nieżla bil-mod mal-blat jaħraq sakemm waslet fit-tarf. Neżgħet is-sandli u tefgħet saqajha fil-baħar. Kien frisk u ħassitu dieħel bħal xafra ġo laħamha. Tbissmet. Qamet bilwieqfa u mxiet ftit iżjed. Il-blat ma kienx jiżloq wisq u l-baħar tant kien nadif li setgħet tara sewwa fejn qed tmidd il-pass. Imxiet ftit passi oħra sakemm l-ilma wasal sa kuxxtejha u d-dublett kien diġà weħel ma' riġlejha. Il-kesħa tal-baħar kienet qed taqtagħlha nifisha. Baqgħet titbissem. Bdiet ħierġa iktar 'il barra fil-baħar u issa tela' sa sidirha. Il-kesħa tiegħu dratha. Setgħet tibqa' bilwieqfa hemm għal ħin twil. Is-sema fuqha u l-baħar taħtha kienu qed ibennuha f'ikħal bla tarf. Ħasset it-toqla li kellha ftit ilu tielgħa 'l fuq minn rasha u tħalliha vojta u ħafifa. Ma setgħetx tieqaf titbissem. Baqgħet miexja 'l quddiem. L-ilma wasal sa għonqha. L-imsielet inħallu minn ma' widnejha u ntelqu f'wiċċ l-ilma ħdejha u l-ilwien tagħhom tħalltu mal-baħar li għannaq kollox miegħu b'ċafċifa ħelwa.

THE FEMININE VOICE OF MALTA

BEFORE WE SLEEP

CLARE AZZOPARDI

ENGLISH TRANSLATION OF "KONFESSJONIJIET QABEL NORQDU"
TRANSLATED BY ALBERT GATT

before we fall asleep, we often talk about our bodies   1
the tangle of our straw-like hair and tangled
there the drunkenness of a relationship grown old
our eyes   a little more nearsighted peering
at a patchwork of pains filmed over
so that we can no longer see which pocket we left our stories in
our cheeks a smattering of holes in which we've tumbled
losing hope
when no one lowered their hair to let us climb back up
our skin a threadbare sheet
our teeth
     I think
have moved
     a little
         more
in mouths that have a whiff of mildew
like the clothes that have aged on our backs
our legs a swing lugging
cumbersome bellies
     lopsided breasts
our knees drums
sounding a call to our uneven arms
you murmur, *and every bit of you I love*

this is the game we play 2
we count the marks left by the weight we bear
see whose run deepest
and all too often I'm the winner

lying before we fall asleep, we disclose the ordeals 3
of this body barely able to break into dawn
or fall silent
      silent
and often we touch the clotted marks
of our fatigue

like the trees in the city we left
they never aged they tore them down   one by one
because, they said, they'll have a better life elsewhere
this body too
close to being uprooted
taken someplace else

so yesterday you said, half joking
it's time we made up our minds
should we be buried here
or there?

as you do every night, tonight 4
you dress the scars my draining strength has left
suture me whole with sequins plucked
from a night of days committed to souls and the dead
feed me the bones of every man who came before
claiming the right to feel the rib
in order to believe
if he believes

now, a wing is missing the   waist aslant
on this body which used to be more whole
instead, as I do every night, tonight
I find myself beside you
and all at once, your solace pulls me out of true

are you really here with me this evening? 5
I don't answer
I turn my back to you a dawn which cannot break
let you caress me
thinking of the woman who once whispered to me
        that I will never understand what weights we bear
        because I've never borne

I turn to you, surprise you, ask you
if fibroids count, are they not borne in a womb,
mine have multiplied, you see,
there must be five or six, perhaps more
they're all at seven, eight centimetres
isn't that another way to bear?

lying with your cheek against my belly I imagine **6**
that you're expecting me to birth water in the form of some weird creature
why not a walk along the canal hand in hand?

some of it makes sense **7**
in our confessions before we fall asleep
and some of it is startling

you always know exactly when it's time
to leave the sheets balled up
beside the bed

you take a blanket
I another
we amble down to the dirty old canal
not far from where we now live
        spread
                lie down
           let go   allow
the chill to weigh us down, bear into us

my toes wander, seeking out yours

> *In this poem, I set out to explore the changes in my body, its frailties and vulnerabilities. Certain changes come unbidden; sometimes they are beyond my grasp. A blemish seems to expand, an ache intensifies and spreads. Wounds I thought had closed reopen, and old memories are reborn. Now, in my late forties, there is more bulk, more awkwardness, more ugliness. A woman's body isn't always beautiful. And that doesn't matter. If I must reveal my body, let it be in its entirety, just as it is, just as I perceive it. Hence, this poem. During long, sleepless nights, I scrutinise my body, trying to embrace all its transformations and bear a weight that I have never borne before. I don't always face this alone. Should I? On the other side of the bed, there is my husband. He listens to my pain and tries to understand my body, not always successfully. When he can't understand, he usually suggests something apparently trivial. "Take a walk by the canal," for example. And yet, it almost always turns out to be more than I could have asked for.*

KONFESSJONIJIET QABEL NORQDU

CLARE AZZOPARDI

ORIGINAL MALTESE VERSION OF "BEFORE WE SLEEP"

qabel norqdu, nitkellmu fuq ġisimna spiss
fuq xagħarna mberfel żbul maqbud
fih is-sokor ta' relazzjoni xiħa
għajnejna   kemm kemm iktar mijopiċi
iħarsu lej' l-irqajja' t'uġigħ miż-żlieġ
li bih ma nagħrfux liema but ħallejna ġrajjietna fih
ħaddejna ħofra ħdejn ħofra, tlifna t-tamiet
minn meta waqajna fihom
u ħadd ma niżżel xagħru biex nitilgħu
il-ġilda liżar li tilfet il-fibri
snienna
         naħseb
li ċċaqalqu
     ftit
        ieħor
minn ħalqna riħa ta' sorra
bħal ħwejjiġna li qdiemu fuqna
riġlejna bandla tqandel
żaqq goffa
      sider żbilanċjat
irkupptejna tnabar
isejħu lil idejna mxattra
tfesfisli, *u nħobbok kollok kemm int*

1

saret logħba din li 2
ngħoddu l-marki tat-toqol
naraw ta' min l-iktar fondi
u ħafna drabi nirbaħ jien

qabel norqdu, nimteddu nqerru l-keded 3
ta' dal-ġisem li mgħadux jiflaħ jisbaħ
jew jiskot
       jiskot
u spiss immissu b'idejna l-għeja mmarkata
ċappa ċappa

bħas-siġar tal-belt mnejn tlaqna
flok xjaħu qaċċtuhom   waħda waħda
għax qalu band'oħra jgħixu aħjar
dan ġisimna wkoll
wasal biex jinqala' mill-għeruq
u jittieħed f'imkien ieħor

ilbieraħ għedtli b'nofs ċajta
trid niddeċiedu fejn se nindifnu
jekk hux hawn
jew hemm!

bħal kull lejl'oħra, illejla **4**
ddewwili l-marki tal-filġa
iġġonġini b'sekwini misruqa lil-lejl
f'dal-jiem tal-erwieħ u l-mejtin
titmagħni l-għadam ta' kull raġel li ġie qablek
u bi dritt mess il-kustilja
għax ried jibda jemmen
jekk jemmen

issa, dan ġisem b'ġewnaħ nieqes   qadd żlugat
seta' xi darba kien iktar shiħ
minflok, bħal kull lejl'oħra, illejla
ninġabar ħdejk
u f'salt, wensek jobromni

kemm int miegħi llejla? **5**
ma nwiġbekx
intik dahri għodwa li ma tafx kif taqbad tisbaħ
inħallik tmellisni
waqt li naħseb fil-mara li darba lissnitli
        li hemm toqol u toqol
        li jien ma nifhimx għax ma ġarrejtx

indur fuqek, naħsdek, nistaqsik jekk
il-fibromi li nġorr jgħoddux daqs ġarr fil-ġuf
għax dan l-aħħar żdiedu
saru ħamsa, sitta, ank'iktar
kollha jkejlu mas-seba', tmien ċentimetri
din mhix tqala wkoll?

b'ħaddek fuq żaqqi nisthajlek tistennieni 6
niled l-ilma f'forma ta' kreatura stramba
għax mhux mixja mal-kanal id f'id?

hemm dak li jagħmel sens 7
fil-konfessjonijiet qabel norqdu
u hemm dak li jissorprendi

int tagħraf eżatt il-waqt li fih
għandna nħallu l-friex
kobba biswit is-sodda

taqbad kutra
jien kutr'oħra
nimxu bil-mod sal-kanal antik, maħmuġ
ftit bogħod mnejn ngħixu issa
    nifirxu
             nimteddu
      nintelqu   inħallu
t-toqol tal-ksieħ jidħol fina

subgħajja ta' saqajja jiġru jfittxu 'l tiegħek

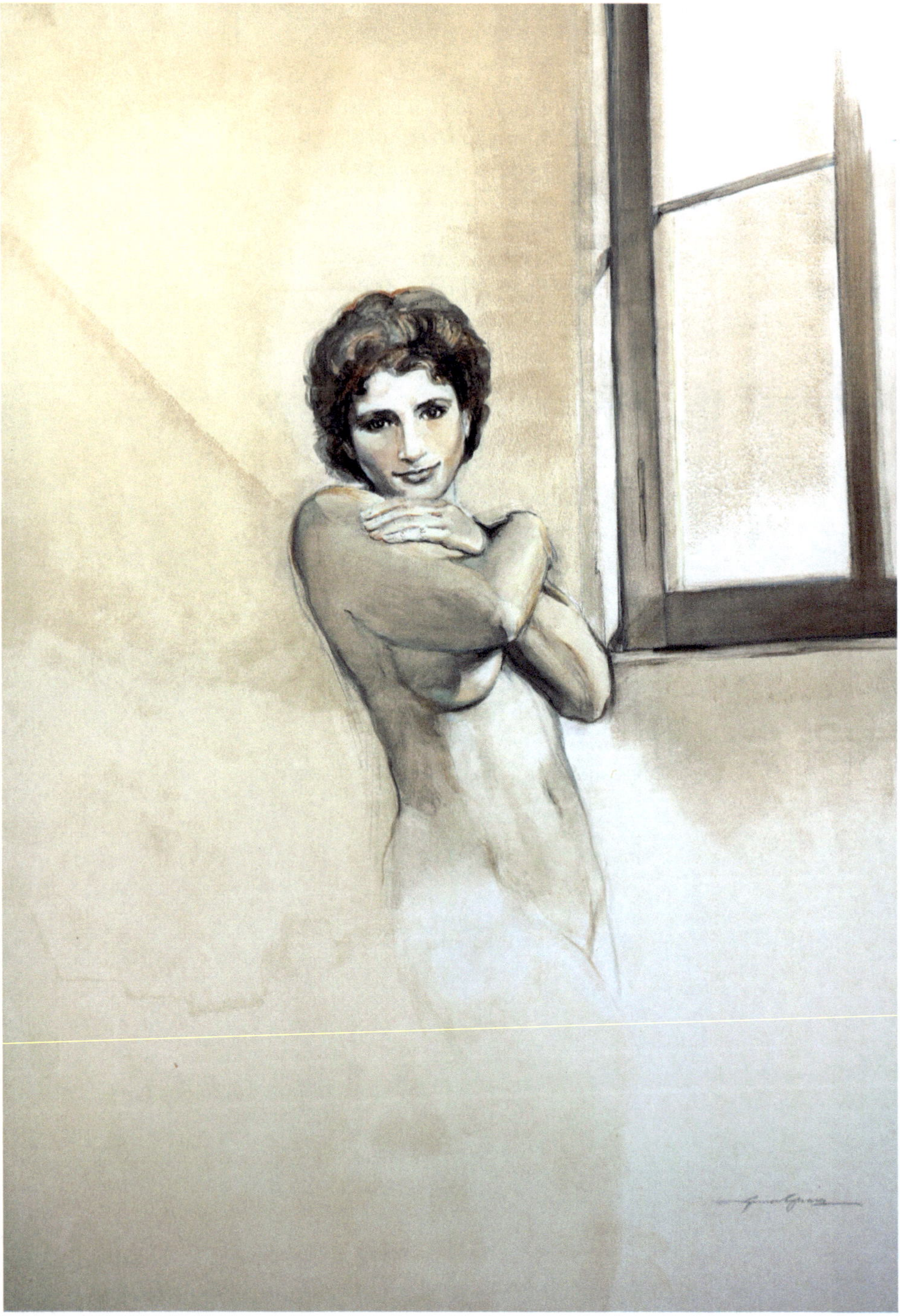

MARIJA IS-SEWDA

ANNA GRIMA

ACRYLIC ON CANVAS 140 X 100 CM. PRIVATE COLLECTION

This painting is of Marija Grech, a 29-year-old mother, barmaid, and prostitute, who was a victim of intimate femicide in 1970. Nicknamed Marija is-Sewda, she was found dead in the bathtub at her house in Strada Fontana, her naked body mutilated by a knife. The murderer was an American sailor, Huston Eustace Featherstone, 19, of Chester, Pennsylvania who met Marija at a bar where she was working.

To create this work, I referred to Delitti f'Malta, by Edward Attard, and George Cini's 2012 publication Strada Stretta, (published by Allied Newspapers). I thus developed a large work on canvas from a small portrait photo, depicting her naked, and holding her breasts (where she was stabbed multiple times). The painting was exhibited during the inaugural collective of 'Strada Stretta – Splendid', in 2011. The exhibition was part of a European project to create 'Incubators for Cultural Enterprises' in six Unesco World Heritage cities.

I was inspired to paint this piece to draw attention to the barbaric reality of femicide through the victim Marija Grech's voice; as well as to take a stand for legislative access against femicide.

**Rajtni liebsa, rajtni mneżża,
iżda lili qatt ma rajtni.**

You've seen me dressed, you've seen me naked,
but you never saw ME.

**Kont nafdak b'għajnejja magħluqin.
Iżda issa, nibża' ngħalaqhom.**

I used to trust you blindly,
but now, I am afraid to close my eyes.

**M'għandhomx ghalfejn imissuk
biex tħossok daqslikieku missuk.**

You don't have to be touched,
to feel like you were.

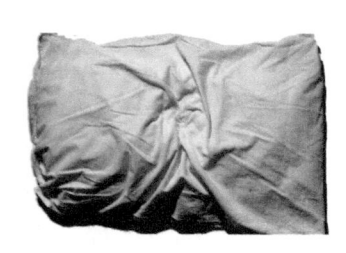

THE WEIGHT OF THEIR SILENCE

JAHEL AZZOPARDI

'The Weight of their Silence' *observes victims' objectification and their silence, whether by choice or by force, and the consequences that follow. Often victims are silent due to a societal pressure to disregard their experiences, taking away their agencies. This project is aimed at offering liberation to those who feel ignored, ridiculed, and blamed. The visual project is presented through imagery, text, and physical artifacts to engage with the viewers and invite them to understand the different scenarios that victims find themselves in.*

The use of objects rather than victims themselves aims to create a space where the victim is not looked at and therefore removed from judgment.

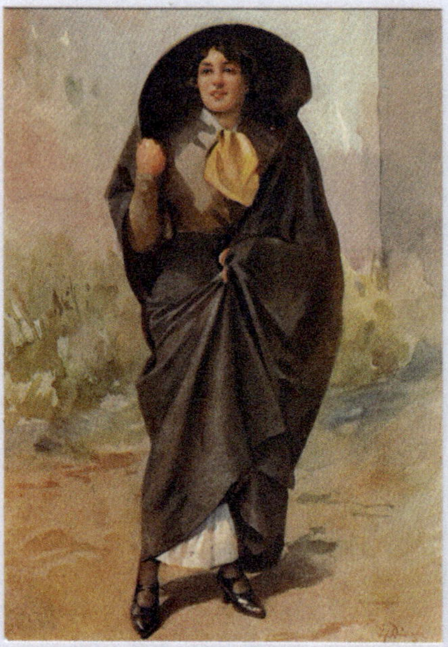

GHONNELLA: DIVERGENT VIEWS

VERONICA VEEN

The following commentary is an excerpt from Veronica Veen's 2020 book Lucija Tells… Women's History and Experience of Life in Gozo. *The multifarious nature of Veen's fieldwork since 1986 and her publications, feature female voices directly from the "field," critical use of her sources, and independent theorizing. All this is to shed the brightest light possible on women's history and their experience of life in Malta, especially in rural Gozo.*

This is how the painter in the 1920's sees it:

The loveliness of the village beauty is displayed to the best advantage in the "national female costume", the *faldetta*. Especially, of course, when she stands before him gracefully and carelessly lifts up the sides of that cloak, together with her skirt, to reveal a bit of lace from her petticoat and her adorable little feet.

The Victorian traveller is carried away in his diary. "The women of all classes wear the *faldetta*, a sort of short cloak that is gathered into plaits on one side only. […] They are always black and the material is either of cotton or silk, according to the means of the wearer. It is a most becoming costume, and shows off the handsome features of the women to great advantage: and they are handsome, almost without exception, combining the fine eyes and hair of Italian beauties with clear complexions. […] The beautiful women of Malta were [sometimes] dressed in their holiday costumes, black silk petticoats being added to the graceful faldetta, the most becoming of all headdresses."

The scholar can not control his curiosity about the origin of the phenomenon. Is the faldetta derived from the Arabian veil, or on the contrary, from the Sicilian manto?

Aside the fact that either could be the case, it might be relevant to ask someone who wore this garment, which by the way is ordinary known as għonnella, for her experiences.

The wearer, aged 77 [in 1988], remembers vividly:

I used to go to church with the għonnella in my hands. I used to put the għonnella on my head at the door of the church. I used to hear Mass and come out [and take it off again.] [This was the custom in Gozo; in Malta the women did it differently.]

Then after some time, I went to live in Malta because I got married and went to stay in Malta. I had two children and I was always going here and there with the għonnella on my head: shopping at the market with the għonnella on my head, a bag hanging from my hand, a child in my arm there, while holding another by the hand, and the għonnella continually falling down, just falling down! And I used to find it very hard!

While travelling on the bus, men used to tell me, as they used to tell every woman wearing the għonnella, while travelling in the bus from Valletta with the għonnella falling down like this, there was always a man to tell me: "will you put that għonnella away, because it is on top of me and it is covering me completely?" And I used to pull slightly the għonnella this way, and I used to sit at the very edge longing desperately to reach home as soon as possible. My hands used to ache so much [to swap him] and I used to suffer so much that I was always ready to go back home!

In the afternoon I used to go shopping again: still wearing my għonnella. I had two boys whom I used to leave with my husband while shopping with my għonnella; buying vegetables, cabbages, cauliflowers. For this kind of shopping I had another għonnella, because I used to wear the new one only for Valletta and the old one for shopping at the greengrocer's. Otherwise I would have spoiled the new one while holding the red pumpkin against my għonnella.

The confrontation of these diverse points of view clarifies my position as a cultural anthropologist using the method of 'participant observation', who is an art historian at the same time, avid to analyse visual information in a historical context. That was also my motivation at the time to publish these testimonies in my Female Images, 1994, just like I include these juxtapositions again in the present book.

Obviously the first three views represent three forms of what we would call now *the male gaze*. The painter and the traveller regard the phenomenon in front of them merely in aesthetical terms, reducing the woman within the costume to an object as well. The scholar does in fact the same in his 'objective' way. Astonishing enough, in spite of a scientifically much more elaborate discourse, this is basically still the way the ghonnella is recently dealt with in a prestigious heritage magazine. The writer does this unfortunately again without any reference to my 1994-publication, that could have enabled him to complete his story with the other side of the coin.

My objective or 'mission', as simple as it actually is, has always been *"to let as many women as possible speak for themselves, which is certainly at least as informative as what has been written about them up to now. A multitude of data never published before, appeared to emerge easily from their rich experience"*, as I jaunty wrote in my *Female Images of Malta; Goddess, Giantess, Farmeress*, 1994.

What we learn from Guza, the wearer, is among many other things, how extremely awkward and troublesome wearing and handling this *"most becoming costume"* was, how it hindered a woman's freedom of movement and even discouraged her going out, intrinsically a downright paradox, because one had to wear the ghonnella to be able to go out altogether. Furthermore, the differences in wearing on Gozo and Malta, and that there were more than one kind of them for different occasions.

Only recently, 2019, I heard a shocking story from Gianna - in the middle of our conversations, so unfortunately not literally recorded - that all the more brings down the roseate dream of the 'male gaze'.

> Retold in my words: *a young girl was sent by her mother to her elder sister, who was on the verge of giving birth, to help her in the house. The husband of the pregnant sister abused the girl, making her pregnant as well. In order to cover this up, in two senses, the little sister was kept inside her mother's house and sent every Sunday to church, 'safely' wrapped up in an ghonnella to prevent any gossip or scandal…*

(And we have to bear in mind that the baby of the young girl will enter the world as the umpteenth child of her mother!)

Last but not least I can mention my own experience with that *"most becoming garment"*. When I tried it on in a courtyard, it was nearly impossible to keep it decently on, already in a little bit of wind.

It is very paradoxical to see how nowadays during many a folkloristic re-enactment, the male gaze of this decorative serenity is still evoked without any consciousness of women's history and experience of life.

THE FEMININE VOICE OF MALTA

THE AMENITY OF SOCIETY

BRENDA PRATO

ENGLISH TRANSLATION OF" IL-KUMDITÀ TAS-SOĊJETÀ"

Because you are a girl,
politely you must converse
and put on a proper dress.
You love dolls, assumably,
but an altar girl you cannot be.

Because you are now a teen,
a tattoo is no option for you,
nor an earring anywhere on you.
Alcohol you cannot touch,
nor let a boy kiss you, hush hush.

Because you are a woman,
Make sure that you serve warm meals,
because only you can manage it all.
Ensure ironed clothes and a tidy house,
since your pension everybody vows.

Since I am a woman,
I've learnt to adapt to societal needs,
how to turn an hour into a quarter,
how to fuse studies and raise babies,
how to wed my job and housework duties.

It is tough to be a woman,
everybody needs you; young and old,
your relatives, your in-laws and your offspring.
What shines forth is what you do not conclude,
then, you, the Church does not include.

But I am a woman,
A daughter, a mother and a wife.
To me, they mean more than a priceless gem.
There is nothing I won't do for them,
because my heart is now in them.

Yet, the woman will always remain a woman.
An individual with rights,
who although commanded by all,
without her there would be no society,
let alone amenity.

We live in a time where human rights are at the forefront of our conversations — on the news, in the streets, in our homes — and these include women's rights. From what I constantly experience as a woman, we still have a long way to go. The woman is usually noticed when the societal needs which are expected of her, are not fully met. On the other hand, no one really asks what the woman, as an individual, legal, and spiritual being, wants. It is not easy to be a mother, a wife, a housewife, a daughter, a student and a Catholic Church expert all at the same time.

This poem briefly goes into the societal expectations throughout a woman's life stages (particularly in Malta in the 1990s) and it demonstrates that ultimately, a woman's heart is her motivating force. She is tired of what is imposed on her yet she loves the people around her so much that she does it anyway out of force of love. The poem ends with a tough statement that society needs to understand to take care of the woman as the woman she actually is, because without the woman, there would not be a society, nor would there be commodity. Society needs to understand this before it is too late.

IL-KUMDITÀ TAS-SOĊJETÀ

BRENDA PRATO

MALTESE TRANSLATION OF "THE AMENITY OF SOCIETY"

Għax inti tifla,
trid titkellem sewwa
u tilbes dublett xieraq
nassumu li tħobb il-pupi
imma abbatina tkun inutli.

Għax inti tfajla,
ma tistax tagħmel tpinġija
Jew misluta fuq ġismek
Lanqas l-alkoħol m'għandek tmiss
Jew tbus ġuvni nkiss nkiss.

Għax inti mara,
Qis li ssajjar dak il-platt sħun
Għaliex ħadd ħliefek ma jlaħħaq
Qis li d-dar tnaddaf u l-ħwejjeġ tistira
Ħalli l-pensjoni jkollok meta tirtira.

La jiena mara,
Tgħallimt nadatta għas-soċjetà
Kif siegħa nġibha kwarta
Kif inrabbi u nistudja f'daqqa
U kif l-faċendi tad-dar u x-xogħol inlaqqa.

Diffiċli tkun mara,
Kulħadd irid minnek
Niesek, niesu u uliedek
Jidher l-iktar dak li ma tagħmilx
Imbagħad fil-Knisja ma tiswix.

Imma jiena mara,
Jiena bint, omm u ta' żewġi
Inħobbhom daqs dawl għajnejja
U kollox nagħmel għalihom
Għax qalbi tinsab fihom.

Però l-mara tibqa' l-mara,
Individwu bid-drittijiet
Li għalkemm kulħadd jikmandha
Mingħajrha la jkun hawn is-soċjetà
U wisq inqas l-kumdità.

THE TALE OF MARJANNA (ONCE MORE)

LEANNE ELLUL

ENGLISH TRANSLATION OF "IL-ĠRAJJA TA' MARJANNA (MILL-ĠDID)"

WHAT NOBODY KNOWS is how much she meant to me.

I'm Marjanna. Marjanna Cumbu. Marjanna Cumbu, from Mosta. Born in 1506. After Nanna Marija, they named me, and Nanna Anna. Marija's my father's mother. Ġulju's my father. Ġulju the juror: Julius Cumbu. A criminal lawyer, he was. And a juror at the Universitas, in Mdina. The local government at the time, that is. So, Marija's my father's mother. And Anna, my mother's mother, Vitor. Not that a lot of people knew her by name. They mostly knew her as the juror's wife. As if there was one juror to begin with. They used to love Mama and Papa. Everybody loved them. They were decent people with the rich and the poor. There were a lot back then, both rich and poor. Maltese people, foreigners. There was nothing to despise in them.

You see, my father had a larger-than-usual appetite, and my mother loved gossiping more than anything else. But who doesn't love a good stew? I, for one. I never wanted to eat meat, and my father could never understand this strange behaviour of his only daughter. And who doesn't speak more than they should about this and that? I'm guilty of that as well. I used to detest gossiping or prying into people's lives, and my mother almost took it personally, assuming I didn't want to share anything with her. The truth is I simply didn't care about idle talk. What did it matter if Ġulina married Patist or Anġlu? Or how many children Kelina had? It didn't interest me at all.

Mama and Papa had it good. Grandmama's and grandpapa's names suited me like they did: Marjanna, for Marija and Anna. It sort of sounds good. There were times when I dreamt of what I would have become should my name have been Sużanna or Mikelina, Luċija or Ilwiża. But I'm a Marjanna now, and I didn't have the worst of days as a young Marjanna. Playing with my friends, the boys, in the valleys of Mosta. There were days when Papa wanted to feed me some pork shank or some animal's breast, and other days when Mama wanted to bring out of me never-ending stories of day and night of which I knew nothing. Wandering in my mind's thoughts is what I used to do. Those thoughts used to take me on long walks on my own. Those walks by which I used to live countless hours on a different land from the same spot, sometimes wandering at the ceiling, other times at the mirror.

Stories often depicted me as beautiful and pure, emphasising my beauty above all else. I heard this portrayal many times, and it often felt like they were talking about someone else. What does it mean to be beautiful? Is it defined by full lips, thick eyebrows, or rounded hips? The stories spoke at length about the traits of a beautiful woman, mostly narrated by men. However, my lips were never full, and my eyebrows and hips neither. To me, there was only one truly beautiful woman.

I spent my childhood playing in the fields and exploring the valley surrounding our family's tower, Torri Cumbo. The tower has been in our family for ages, and I often wonder how many generations the tradition of its name dates back to. When I was born, my father had hoped for a boy to carry on the family surname. Torri Cumbo of the Cumbo family. Well, the tower is a villa, really. Imposing, to say the least, with its windows, doors, arches, and enclaves overlooking stunning views of acres of lush green in scent, of mornings the colour of muteness, and evenings of softness. Till the land would be assaulted and every man and woman made a slave.

What a beautiful tower it was, especially its surroundings. The large reservoir led to Chadwick Lakes through an underground canal, and there were gardens everywhere. I often got lost wandering through our gardens until I remembered our family's tomb from the Roman Era. Then, soon enough, I would often find myself wandering through the narrow alleys of thought and passages of ponder.

Countless hours of breeze the smell of thyme and rosemary, sage and saffron. They were anything but happy that I would wander off like that, mostly because of the attacks by the Turks. Once or twice I was punished for wandering off. And for every hour spent walking away from the tower, I would spend two days locked. During one of the walks, one of the rare few, as quick as possible,

I went threading the path where one valley meets another. On that day, I saw Toni. Toni Manduca. Born in 1504, I later discovered. Son of the Baron, though I still didn't know he was his son. There was a thin young lady with him, short and puny. Her face catching reflections of the sun's light, and her eyes, even from a side, I could see them glimmer. I had told Stilla about her, one of our servants who supposedly used to know everything about everyone and with whom Mama used to chew the fat. As soon as I told her how long the young lady's hair was, her face tender, she gave me her word on her Lord that he was the Baron's son, and the girl, she should have been his sister.

This young lady and the man had caught my eye in May. Stilla was quick to go and tell Mama that I mentioned Toni as if I liked him, not because I was curious about them. Stilla thinks she knows everything, but she doesn't. Mama went to tell Papa and in the blink of an eye, both fathers agreed to marry us in August. I'm not sure how everything happened so hastily.

I never understood this, how I could live my whole life with someone, for better, for worse, until death do us apart without knowing what he loved to eat, what bothered him, or what he dreamt of. And I couldn't speak to Toni if we weren't accompanied by someone, at our tower, in church, on Sundays, for mass. Most of the time his sister used to come with him. On those days our meetings weren't so bad.

At our tower then, there was Ħaġġi. He started to work for us three years prior. He was baptised, this Ħaġġi, and Papa started to like him a lot. As much as I used to speak with Stilla, I started to speak with him too. Little by little, one word led to another, and at that time he started to show up even more. Sometimes he used to keep an apple for me, one he would have cut from the garden. And I would make him a pie with that same apple — I who always loved to cook. I was trying to understand myself and what I wanted. And Ħaġġi used to make me dream and go to places afar, farther than ever, even if standing in the same corner.

Until an idea sprang to mind during one of my endless walks. Ħaġġi should pretend that he kidnapped me. That's what he had to do, of course. It was no big deal considering how many and how frequently prisoners used to be kidnapped. The plan was to go to his land together. And I knew there were going to be days when I wanted my mama's embrace and others when I longed for Papa's touch, you see. But what I was trying to understand Mama and Papa could never figure out. No matter how much they loved Ħaġġi, Papa could never understand if there was to be a bond between us. Ħaġġi, a slave. I, the daughter of a juror.

Endless stories, there were, about Ħaġġi who had sworn to take a Maltese girl in the King of Barbaria's harem. Endless stories, there were, about promised money. Endless stories, there were, about distant oaths. And when closer to August they started to adorn the tower as our wedding — Toni's and myself — was approaching, they prepared the flowers and the wheat and the hazelnuts to throw them upon us. The day was soon approaching then when at two in the morning Ħaġġi had to knock on the door of our quarters. I had already prepared a bundle of clothes and other necessities and hid them under the bed. That evening, I had sent Stilla to fetch me a glass of water and I went to sleep fully clothed. There were days when I sent her to get a glass of water so that I could observe her coming back and try to understand what drew me to her, with her walk almost a dance, while she used to put me to sleep and kiss me on the forehead. It wasn't the gossip that drew me to her, God forbid. And yet there were nights when I dreamt of her. That evening, when she came back, I pretended I was fast asleep, even though I didn't sleep at all. A few hours later, a knock.

I heard Rafel, our other servant, that is scurrying toward the door, asking who was there. Ħaġġi said it was him, and Rafel didn't think twice. He opened the door. On that day, Ħaġġi wasn't meant to be alone, either. Little did I expect he would bring a clan of 60 Turks, or so. And yet, he did. I'm not sure whether it was believable or not. I mean, I had told Ħaġġi to put a handkerchief around my mouth. There was no other way for others to believe it was true. And while every Turk wreaked havoc in our home, Ħaġġi and I fled to the seashore.

They told many stories the way they wanted, of how much the Turks stole from Wied il-Għasel, and how much money and gold they took with them. And it is true that they broke a lot of chairs, flipped many tables, and cut off bouquets of flowers, but it's not true that they killed a servant with a dagger and slid the guest's throats open. Ħaġġi seemed to want me, and he did what he had to do. Then, we took off from Selmun, daylight calling us from Tripoli. Mama and Papa broke my heart, as expected. I could imagine Mama crying as loud as she could, praying and praying, and Papa, I could close my eyes and see him beat himself up for it. Back then though, I didn't see another way out. And neither did I comprehend myself completely.

On that day, the people of Mosta left their homes. Every single person left theirs to come to ours, to save me, to bring me back. They say, Mikiel, a guy from Mosta, came back panting telling them he had met us at Salini. But when they arrived we had already almost reached Tripoli. They said, time and time again, that I was scared and afraid. Well, I was a bit scared, but not enough to hold me back. They took care of me and saw to my demands.

When we arrived in Tripoli, we made our way to the palace, where Ħaġġi lived for many years. They gave me lots of damask, silver, and gold; I didn't inquire about their origin, and perhaps it's all for the better. And I slept, deep sleep, throughout day and night, like I have never slept before. Back in Malta, I heard that Toni couldn't find any solace. My heart somewhat ached seeing that Toni wasn't all that bad, but what was I supposed to do? My heart was never drawn to him. Toni had decided to come to Tripoli. He was never a man for someone to meddle with — least of all, Ħaġġi.

Ħaġġi and I spoke at length, but it seemed that we didn't discuss everything. About my beliefs and my ways. I assumed that since he had been baptised, he would continue to believe in our God. But Ħaġġi made it clear about that — he had to return to his God and I was to do the same. I started to confide in Asseba, the king's daughter. Born in 1511, she was. And so beautiful she defied my prior understanding of beauty. Unlike Ħaġġi, who more than once lifted a hand on me, called me names and put me to shame, Asseba showed me otherwise. She heard and understood. There was something in Asseba that I wanted more than the damask, all the silver and gold.

With Asseba, I started to meet for long walks, like those of Mosta, the ones of Malta. We laughed when she told me that, like me, she didn't want to eat meat anymore. With Asseba, the tree's green looked more verdant, the sand's white looked paler, and the sky's blue looked even bluer. With Asseba, I could dream with no tomorrow, with no man's hand snatching me, closing me into a fist, and dictating what I should and shouldn't do. We just had to make sure Majjena, her friend Majjena, wasn't looking — and for that moment, for just one moment, we could be ourselves.

When Toni arrived in Tripoli, being the wise man that he was, he started to make friends here and there, always making his way to inner circles, singing in the majestic halls of the kings. Once, during a great feast, he saw me and walked toward me. He was shaking and sweating. He took me aside, discreetly almost. He told me what we had to do to flee from there. But I didn't want to go back to Malta. Now that I had found Asseba I knew what I truly wanted and I couldn't go back with him, under the eyes of Stilla and the inquisitive look of my mother. Stories said that I came back to Malta, that I fled there dressed like a Turk, and that not long after I died in the arms of Dun Ambrog.

But my story and that of Asseba continued in other lands, far away. One evening, like a couple of months before, we fled the palace. On that day, Asseba and I fled away from everyone, together. We led a life of silence, away from everything, a difficult life without any gold or pearls. We became the dark of those rough days. How much we walked, I cannot remember, but we walked for days on end. There were days when we cried, yet together. The world wasn't going to understand. We were far better off without Toni and Ħaġġi, away from Majjena and the king, away from Mama and Papa, away from all stories and legends.

And what nobody knows is how much she meant to me.

IL-ĠRAJJA TA' MARJANNA (MILL-ĠDID)

LEANNE ELLUL

ORIGINAL MALTESE VERSION OF "THE TALE OF MARJANNA (ONCE MORE)"

LI ĦADD MA JAF HU kemm kienet saret tfisser għalija.

Jiena Marjanna. Marjanna Cumbu. Marjanna Cumbu l-Mostija. Tal-1506 jiena. Għan-nanna Marija msemmija, u għan-nanna Anna. Marija omm il-papà, Ġulju. Ġulju l-ġurat. Julius Cumbu. Avukat tal-Kriminal kien il-papà. U ġurat l-Università tal-Imdina wkoll. Il-Gvern lokali jiġifieri. Mela Marija omm il-papà. U Anna, omm il-mamà, Vitor. Mhux għax ħafna kienu jafuha b'isimha lill-mamà. Iktar kienu jafuha bħala mart il-ġurat. Bħallikieku ġurat wieħed kien hawn. Kienu jħobbuhom lill-mamà u 'l-papà ta. Kulħadd kien iħobbhom. Għax il-mamà u l-papà kienu jimxu ta' nies mas-sinjur u mal-fqir. Mit-tnejn kien hawn qabda. Maltin, barranin. Ftit li xejn kien hemm li tista' tmaqdar fihom.

Ara, biex inkun qed ngħid kollox, il-papà kien żaqqieq iżżejjed u l-mamà tiha zzekzek u ttiha xejn iżjed. Imma min ma taqagħlux żaqqu għal laħam l-istuffat? Jiena, fil-fatt, minn daqshekk. Qatt ma ridt niekol laħam u l-papà ma seta' qatt jifhimha din l-istramberija ta' bintu l-waħdanija. U min kultant kelma żejda ma jgħidhiex fuq dik u l-oħra? Jiena wkoll. Kont nobgħod ngħid fuq in-nies jew imqar nosservahom u l-mamà bħal kienet tkun se taħbat teħodha kontrija u taħsibni ma rridx naqsam magħha dak li naf. Ħlief li jien, ma kont inkun naf xejn, għax lanqas biss kien jimpurtani. X'differenza kienet se tagħmilli lili Ġulina żżewġitx lil Patist jew lil Anġlu? Jew Kelina kemm kellha tfal? Fejn naf kemm kellha tfal jiena? Kellhiex sitta u kellhiex tmienja u kellhiex għaxra, fejn kont bqajt.

Ġiethom tajba 'l-mamà u 'l-papà, li isem nannieti seta' jingħadli hekk. Marjanna. Għal Marija u Anna. Donnu jdoqqli. Kien hemm drabi meta ħlomt kif kont inkun kieku ismi kien Sużanna jew Mikelina. Luċija jew Ilwiża. Imm'issa Marjanna ġejt, u ma kellix jiem mill-agħar bħala ċ-ċkejkna Marjanna. Nilgħab ma' sħabi s-subien fil-widien tal-Mosta. Kien hemm jiem li fihom il-papà ried jitmagħni kemm-il xikel u sider ta' xi annimal, u jiem oħra li fihom il-mamà riedet ixxoqqli minni kemm-il storja dwar lejl u nhar li dwarhom m'aft ebda tarf. Iktar kont insibni nhewden u nintilef fi ħrejjef moħħi, dawk li kienu jeħduni fuq mixjiet twal. Waħdi. Jew dawk li bihom kont ngħix sigħat f'art oħra mill-istess imkien, kultant inħares lejn is-saqaf, kultant lejn mera.

Fl-istejjer jgħidu li kont sabiħa, sa li kont qisni fjura jgħidu, u safja, u jinsistu li sabiħa ħafna. Din li sabiħa ħafna smajtha fuq li smajtha. Jibqgħu jgħidu li sabiħa ħafna u qisni nħoss li qed jitkellmu fuq xi oħra. Għax xi jkun sabiħa, hux ix-xufftejn mimlijin, il-ħuġbejn mimlijin għandu mnejn, jew il-ġenbejn. Il-ġenbejn mimlijin vera sbieħ ħafna. Qalu ħafna fl-istejjer, huma, kif tkun mara sabiħa. U dejjem irġiel kienu li qalu ġrajjieti. Imma la xufftejja qatt ma kienu mimlijin, la ħuġbejja u lanqas ġenbejja. U mara sabiħa nett f'għajnejja waħda kien hemm.

Tfuliti fl-għelieqi u l-wied ta' mat-Torri l'għandna. It-Torri Cumbo. Hekk ried isemmih il-papà tal-papà tal-papà … lanqas naf kemm-il papà rridu mmorru lura. Il-papà ma twelidi xtaq bil-bosta li kont tifel biex jitkompla kunjom il-familja. Il-familja Cumbo tat-Torri Cumbo. Villa dat-torri jiġifieri. Imponenti kieku. Kemm twieqi u bibien, arkati u daħliet iħarsu lejn meded art irwejjaħ ħadranija minn lewn l-għodwiet mielsa u l-għaxijiet irtuba. Sakemm l-art tiġi assedjata u jerġgħu jikinsu kemm nisa u rġiel isibu lsira. Imma —

Xi ġmiel ta' torri u l-madwar, l-iktar il-madwar. Il-ġibjun daqsiex li jagħti għal Wied il-Qlejgħa minn kanal taħt l-art u l-ġonna fuq ġonna. Kemm-il darba ntlift indur fil-ġonna tagħna stess sakemm niftakar fit-tomba tal-familja. Tal-Era Rumana mid-dehra. Malajr nitgerrex imbagħad u nerġa' nintilef fil-mogħdijiet tal-ħsieb u t-trejqiet tat-thewdin.

Sigħat shaħ fewġa ta' sagħtar u ldin, salvja u żagħfran. Xejn ma kienu jieħdu pjaċir li nitbiegħed daqstant, ħabba l-ħbit mit-Torok l-iktar, u ġieli qlajtha. U ta' siegħa sewwa li ndum miexja lil hinn mit-torri kont naqla' jumejn ġewwa. F'waħda mill-mixjiet lil hinn, f'waħda mill-ftit u bil-moħbi u ta' malajr, mort interraq, fejn wied jingħaqad ma' ieħor. Dakinhar rajt lil Toni. Toni Maduca. Tal-1504, skoprejt iktar tard. Bin il-Baruni li kont għadni ma nafx li kien ibnu. Miegħu kien hemm tfajla dakinhar, qsajra u rqajqa. Wiċċha jaqbad dawl ix-xemx u għajnejha, anke mill-ġenb, stajt narahom ileqqu. Kont għedt lil Stilla fuqha, waħda mis-sefturi li taparsi kienet tkun taf fuq kollox u fuq kulħadd u l-mamà spiss kienet tħabbat kelma magħha. U lanqas ilħaqt għedtilha kif it-tfajla xagħarha twil u wiċċha tari, li ma tatnix il-kelma tagħha fuq Alla li ħalaqha, li dak bin il-Baruni u dik ta' miegħu, għandu mnejn kienet oħtu.

Dakinhar li lmaħthom lil dit-tfajla u ta' magħha kien Mejju. Stilla kienet pronta marret tgħid lill-mamà li semmejt lil Toni bħallikieku għoġobni u mhux għax sempliċement ġietni kurżità dwarhom. Stilla mingħaliha li taf, u ma taf xejn. Il-mamà kienet marret tiġri tgħid lill-papà u f'kemm trodd salib u nofs, iż-żewġ papajiet ftiehmu li jżewġuna għal Awwissu. Lanqas naf kif kollox ġara daqshekk malajr.

Din qatt ma fhimtha, kif stajt inkun ma' persuna għal ħajti kollha fit-tajjeb u fil-ħażin sa ma l-mewt tifridna meta la kont għadni naf imqar xi tħobb jiekol u xi jdejjaqha jew kemm toħlom. U ma stajtx inkellmu lil Toni jekk mhux b'xi ħadd magħna, jekk mhux fit-torri tagħna, jew il-knisja, nhar ta' Ħadd, għall-quddies. Ħafna drabi kienet tiġi oħtu. Bħal dakinhar il-laqgħat tagħna ma kinux ikunu mill-agħar.

Fit-torri tagħna mbagħad, kien hemm Ħaġġi. Kien daħal magħna xi tliet snin qabel. Tgħammed Ħaġġi u l-papà beda jħobbu tgħidx kemm. Daqskemm kont nitħaddet ma' Stilla, kont bdejt nitħaddet miegħu ftit ftit, u kelma ġġib kelma u dik il-ħabta beda jidher iktar. Kultant iħallili tuffieħa li jkun qata' mill-ġnien. U jien inħallilu torta bl-istess tuffieħa li jkun ħalla hu, jien li minn dejjem kont inħobb insajjar. Kont qed nipprova nifhem lili nnifsi u xi rrid. U Ħaġġi kien iġegħelni noħlom u mmur u ndur imkejjen bogħod u iżjed bogħod, imqar mill-istess rokna.

Sakemm feġġet f'moħħi l-ħolma f'waħda mill-mixjiet bla qies. Ħaġġi kellu jagħmel tabirruħu li ħarrabni. Hekk kellu jagħmel, mela x'inhu. Ma kinitx ħaġa kbira meta tant pringunieri kienu jinsterqu spiss. Flimkien kellna mmorru lil hinn lejn artu. U kont naf li kien se jkun hemm jiem meta nixtieq it-tgħanniqet tal-mamà u kien se jkun hemm jiem meta nixxennaq għafset il-papà, jiġifieri. Imma dak li kont qed nipprova nifhem jiena, la l-mamà u lanqas il-papà ma setgħu qatt jifhmuh. Iħobbu kemm kienu jħobbu lil Ħaġġi, il-papà qatt ma

79

kien se jifhem kieku qatt xtaqt li jkun hemm xi ħaġa bejnietna. Ħaġġi, ilsir. Jiena, bint ġurat.

Kemm stejjer dwar is-Sultan ta' Berberija li Ħaġġi tah kelma li jeħodlu bint Maltija ġewwa l-ħarem. Kemm stejjer dwar flus imwiegħda. Kemm stejjer dwar ħalfiet imbiegħda. U meta għal ħabta ta' Awwissu, kienu bdew iżejnu t-Torri għax kien qorob iż-żmien li niżżewweġ lil Toni, lestew il-fjuri u l-qamħ u l-ġellewż biex jiftgħuh fuqna. Kien qorob sew il-jum meta xis-sagħtejn ta' filgħodu Ħaġġi kellu jħabbat il-bieb tal-kwartier tagħna. Jien kont ilħaqt ħejjejt sorra ħwejjeġ u bżonnijiet oħrajn u ħbejthom taħt is-sodda. Dakinhar lil Stilla kont bgħattha ġġibli tazza ilma u kont dħalt norqod bil-ħwejjeġ b'kollox. Kien hemm jiem meta bgħattha ġġibli tazza ilma biex noqgħod inħares lejha ġejja lura u nipprova nifhem x'qed jiġbidni lejha, bil-mixja tagħha żifna, hi u ddaħħalni fis-sodda u tbusni fuq ngħasi. Żgur ma kienx iz-zekzik li kienet izzekzek li jiġbidni, ma tarax. U kienu ħafna l-iljieli li matulhom ħlomt biha. Dakinhar, meta ġiet lura, lgħabtha li kienet marret għajni bija diġà, anke jekk m'għalaqtx għajn m'għajn. Sakemm ftit sigħat wara, instemgħet it-taħbita.

Kont smajt lil Rafel, qaddej ieħor minn tagħna, iħaffef lejn il-bieb u jistaqsi min hemm. Ħaġġi wieġeb li hu u Rafel ma ħasibhiex u fetaħ. Kif konna tkellimna, dakinhar Ħaġġi ma kellux ikun watdu. Lanqas ma kont bsart li se jġib ġaj ta' sittin Tork ħa jaħbtu għalina. Imma ġabhom. Ma nafx kemm ried jagħmilha tidher ta' vera. Lil Ħaġġi kont għedtlu jiena stess idawwar maktur ma' ħalqi. Ma kienx hemm mod ieħor kif nitwemmnu. U waqt li kull Tork dar iħarbat darna, jien u Ħaġġi ħrabna sax-xatt.

Fl-istejjer qalu kemm serqu mir-raba' ta' Wied il-Għasel, kemm flus u deheb ħadulna. U minnu li kissru s-siġġijiet, u minnu li qalbu xi mwejjed, u minnu li qaċċtu l-bukketti imma mhux minnu li lill-qaddej qatluh b'stallett u li ħanxru mill-ħaddara. Ħaġġi kien jidher li lili jrid, u lili ħa. Imbagħad salpajna minn Selmun mas-sebħ isejħilna minn Tripli.

Il-papà u l-mamà qasmuli qalbi kif stennejt. Lill-mamà bħal stajt nismagħha tixgħer kemm tiflaħ, talba fl-art u oħra fis-sema, u lill-papà stajt nagħlaq għajnejja u narah jagħti fuq rasu. Imma ma deherlix li kien hemm mod ieħor dakinhar. U lanqas ma kont għadni fhimt lili nnifsi sew.

80

Dakinhar il-Mostin qamu u ħarġu minn djarhom. Kull Mosti u Mostija jiġru lejn darna ħa jsalvawni, ħa jġibuni lura. Jgħidu li l-Mosti Mikiel kien wasal jilħeġ u qalilhom li ltaqa' magħna n-naħa tas-Salini. Imma meta waslu x-xatt konna ġa qrobna sew lejn Tripli. Kemm qalu li qalbi kienet imbeżżgħa u mwerwra. Xi ftit imbeżżgħa kont, jiġifieri, imma mhux imbeżżgħa biżżejjed li ma mmurx. Kemm daru bija u raw li ma jonqosni xejn.

Mal-wasla fi Tripli erħejnielha għand is-sultan, fejn Ħaġġi għammar għal ħafna snin. Kemm tawni damask, u deheb u fided, li ma staqsejtx imnejn ġew u jaf imnalla. U rqadt raqda fonda tul il-jum u l-lejl li segwa li bħalha kont ili ma norqod żmien. Lura Malta, smajt li Toni ma seta' jistabar b'xejn. Qalbi ngħasfet ftit għax Toni ma kienx mill-agħar, imma xi stajt nagħmel jekk qalbi qatt ma kienet miġbuda lejh? Toni kien iddeċieda li jiġi lejn Tripli. Ħadd ma kien jilgħab bih lil Toni, aħseb u ara Ħaġġi.

Konna tħadditna sew jien u Ħaġġi imma donnu li mhux dwar kull ħaġa. Dwar x'nemmen u kif nimxi. Kont ħsibt li la hu kien bidel twemminu, mela kien se jibqa' jemmen f'Alla tagħna. Imma Ħaġġi fuq din kien ċar — hu kellu jdur għal Alla tiegħu u jiena kelli nagħmel l-istess. Dan kollu kont bdejt nitħaddtu ma' Asseba, bint is-sultan. Tal-1511, hi. U kienet sabiħa bħalma qatt ma fhimt qabel xi tkun is-sbuħija. Ħaġġi mhux darba jew tnejn refa' idu fuqi, għajjarni u żeblaħni. Asseba wrietni mod ieħor. Semgatni u fehmitni. Kien hemm xi ħaġa f'Asseba li ridtha ferm iżjed mid-damask, mid-deheb u mill-fided.

Ma' Asseba bdejt niltaqa' għal mixjiet bħal dawk tal-Mosta, ta' Malta. Dħaqna meta qaltli li bħali, anke hi, ma tixtieqx kieku tiekol iżjed laħam l-annimali. Ma' Asseba aħdar is-siġar deher iżjed aħdar, abjad ir-ramel deheb iżjed abjad, u ikħal is-sema deher iżjed ikħal. Ma' Asseba stajt noħlom bla għada, bla id ir-raġel taqbadni morsa u tagħfasni ponn u tgħidli x'għandi nagħmel u tikkmandani x'm'għandix nagħmel. Konna biss naraw li naħarbu lil Majjena, Majjena seħbitha, u nkunu aħna għal ftit ħin, imqar ftit ħin biss.

Meta Toni kien leħaq wasal Tripli, ta' makakk li kien, beda jitħabbeb 'l hemm u 'l hawn, u beda diehel fil-qalba, ikanta sa fis-swali maestuzi tas-sultan. Darba waħda, waqt festa kbira, rani u resaq lejja. B'idejh jirtogħdu u l-għaraq iqattar minnu, ħadni f'ġenb. Donnu ma riedx jagħti wisq fil-għajn lanqas. Qalli

81

l-pjan tiegħu kollu, x'kellna nagħmlu biex immur lura miegħu Malta. Imma Malta ma ridtx immur. Issa li kont sibt lil Asseba u kont fhimt verament x'ridt, ma stajtx immur lura Malta, taħt l-għajnejn seqer ta' Stilla, taħt l-għajnejn għarriexa t'ommi. L-istejjer qalu li erġajt lura Malta, li ħrabt liebsa lbies Tork, u anke li mitt ftit wara li ġabuni lura fi ħdan Dun Ambroġ.

Imma l-istorja tiegħi u ta' Asseba kompliet f'artijiet oħra ibgħed. Lejla waħda, bħal ftit xhur qabel, ħrabna mill-palazz. Dik id-darba, jiena u Asseba, ħrabna 'l hinn minn kulħadd, flimkien. Għexna fis-skiet u bogħod min-nies ħajja iebsa u mċaħħda minn kull deheb u ġawhar. Sirna d-dlam ta' dawk il-jiem ħorox. Kemm imxejna nsejna, imma għal jiem fuq jiem, imxejna. Kien hemm drabi meta bkejna, imma flimkien. Id-dinja qatt ma kienet se tifhem. Konna aħjar 'il bogħod minn Toni u Ħaġġi, 'il bogħod minn Majjena u s-sultan, 'il bogħod mill-papà u l-mamà, 'il bogħod mill-istejjer u l-leġġendi.

U li ħadd ma jaf hu kemm kienet saret tfisser għalija.

> *This story is a retelling of the classic Maltese legend of the Bride of Mosta (L-Għarusa tal-Mosta). Through this retelling, Marjanna, the main protagonist, who in the original story was stolen by the Turks and then taken back by her lover Toni only to die once back in Malta, is given agency. She is now the maker of her own stories. Written in first person, this retelling is narrated in her own voice from her own perspective as she recounts what she has been through, the decisions she has taken that led her to where she ended up, and the choices she made given her thoughts and her feelings whom at the time would not have been accepted, neither in Malta nor in Tripoli. The retelling of the story respects as much of the historical elements as possible, whilst intertwining a fresh perspective of the main events recounted in Marjanna's voice with a twist or two at the end.*

IMMACOLATA CONCETTA

LORANNE VELLA

ENGLISH TRANSLATION OF AN EXCERPT FROM "MARTA MARTA"

BENEDITTA'S WORDS have me thinking about the past. Memories are as dear to me as she says they are to her, but I don't feel like they're eluding me. I may have forgotten some of the finer details, yes, while I've added in some others for embellishment. Take the day of the feast dinner at my grandmother's when I was nine years old. What difference does it make if the tablecloth had indeed been white, as I remember it? And if not, then I had also made up the fact that my grandmother used to boil it in water mixed with caustic soda to make it whiter, to help account for her gleaming quality in my own head. I see nothing wrong with forgetting memories sometimes, but what do I know? As long as you don't go looking for them in your mind and find nothing there instead.

Maybe that's what Beneditta was trying to tell me, that she had caught a glimpse of the void and, unlike me, she didn't know how to quickly fill it with something else. Let's face it, even I can grasp that it's no fun for anyone to be looking inwards and to encounter nothing where you were expecting to find something. In my case, not only is there no void when I'm looking back in time, there's an entire mountain of stuff there instead.

This reminds me of Carmelina's habit of walking backwards. I should have suggested Beneditta give it a try. I should encourage all the girls to turn around and try walking backwards. One of these days they'll catch me walking through the corridor backwards, but there's no way any of them would dare call me *granċ*, crab!

I remember the route I travelled to get here intimately, the route Dolor and I traversed together. I have no gaps in my mind when it comes to recalling the endless arguments with my father, from when I taught myself to read the writings of those well-known wise men, and also of those wise women to whom history has been less kind, when my mind turned salty and our thinking on every subject diverged, until the very last day before he died. Heaven and hell, Adam and Eve, mortal sin, venial sin, the Commandments, the Sacraments, and every other belief he held dear — we couldn't agree on any of it. And we carried on bickering so that none of us came out the winner. Because my father had a closed mind, secured with a thousand padlocks and, to make matters worse, he was stubborn too — as stubborn as I was, if not more. I wanted to throw my mind wide open, and so, for every dogma he hurled at me, I hit back with a hundred questions. His reply was always that there wasn't any need for questions: faith was faith, you believed without questioning.

I promise you, his final breath was my first.

Although I still contemplate, to this very day: did he ever find out that there was no heaven waiting for him in the end? My father died, but his closed-minded mentality that avoided all avenues of enquiry followed us everywhere, gagging and stifling every alternative thought before it had a chance to surface.

"I'm choking," I remember telling Dolor.

"We'll turn this world upside together, you'll see," she reassured me.

"Yes," I said, "but how? I'm not a fighter, I wouldn't last five minutes in a battle. An angry mob terrifies me, I'd wet my pants and let them take me, let them trample me in an instant. I'm just not the type to revolutionise the world, to turn it all upside down. I mean, what can I change? I'm powerless. I'd end up bashing my head against the wall instead, smashing it into fragments before successfully changing anything. No..." I continued, "Mine's a different kind of fight. But don't worry that I'm too afraid or that I'm only going to do what I'm told. If something feels too huge to overcome, then I'll start small — I'll get there in the end."

I'm capable of building a tiny world for myself out of everything I like that surrounds me, and to give it a new meaning that makes sense to me. I'm adept at picking and choosing the relevant bits and binning everything else that doesn't matter. I adapt easily to what's around me, of course I do, but if you look more closely, you'll notice that I've adapted it all to suit me, actually. I try to do everything on a small, small scale because in life, you'll never get anywhere if you're too ambitious, so best to start small and get things done, instead of only dreaming. That's my gospel – although I never give up on dreams, which is a story for another day, let it rest for now.

Dolor said, "Leave it up to me, you demolish and rebuild the small stuff, and I'll attack the big stuff myself."

She's a brave one, this Dolor. I still remember how she appeared to me as she was saying these words, the back of her head silhouetted against an orb of bright light, glowing.

"Like a vision of the Madonna," I told her.

"Which one?" she asked.

"You are the Queen of the Angels," I replied. She burst out laughing.

"When are you going to crown me then?"

I've made up my mind. For the coronation of the Madonna this year, I want the new girl, Nathaline. I mentioned to her recently that there are those who believe the Madonna became pregnant with Jesus through her ear, and Nathaline looked puzzled, as if she hadn't understood. I explained that the idea of the Virgin Mary becoming pregnant by being touched between the legs, like every other woman, was so deplorable to certain wise men of the Church, that they decided the mother of God had become aware of the presence of Jesus in her womb when she heard the words of the angel announcing it in her ear. *He planted the seed in her ear*, I told her, *but I'm not sure which one, the left or the right. And so, the Word became flesh because it slipped into Mary's ear.*

Nathaline remained silent, as though she were chewing on my every word. I felt, in that moment, like the angel who'd whispered into her ear, and she was like the Madonna weighing up the meaning of my words. Since then, I haven't stopped thinking about Nathaline in the white dress and blue veil, holding the diadem in her hand and leading the procession with her head bowed towards the statue of the Blessed Virgin in the courtyard. That girl has the face of the Madonna. I realised this the first time I laid eyes on her. I imagined her with the veil on her head, framing her face, like a true and proper reincarnation of the Holy Mary. I haven't disclosed any of this to Dolor yet, but she always leaves this particular feast in my hands. She knows I enjoy it.

At school, on the first of May, we used to prepare a big feast. We would spend the entire year before giddy with anticipation. At the convent of San Ġużepp, where I went to school, they would invite us girls, all dressed in white with a small basket filled with flowers in our hands, and our parents, for the coronation. The most beautiful girl among us that year was chosen to place the crown on the head of the statue of the Madonna. It was a giant statue, bigger, I reckon, than the girl who was tasked with climbing the ladder next to it and placing the crown on its head. I remember the crown vividly, sitting on a square cushion covered in blue velvet, the colour of the sky in springtime, in the hands of the girl leading the procession. I used to be terrified something would happen to make the crown slide off the cushion, or off the head of the Madonna.

At the time, I couldn't decide whether I'd be overjoyed or not if they were to choose me to do the crowning the following year. I'd have been happy, I was sure of that. I used to wish and wish that someday it would be my turn to lead the procession of girls towards the Madonna — me at the front bearing the crown and the other girls behind me, their baskets filled with perfumed petals. At the same time, the fear that the crown would slip from my grip, and that I'd screw up the entire event, tormented me, so I'd tell myself, *No, no, better if they didn't choose me.* Because I liked sitting there in the schoolyard with the other girls, holding the small hymn book, singing the song of our Lady of Lourdes, the Angelus, the Queen of Angels, the Ave Maria, the Hail Mary, You Are the Light, the Morning Star, and the Merciful Mother, teach us to be good, teach us how to love, while observing the full ritual of the coronation from the stalls and praying to our Sovereign and our Mother that I might, as a show of devotion, offer up my eyes, ears, mouth, heart and all of me to her, without holding anything back.

I'd surrender myself into her arms, for her to watch over me, because only then could I breathe more easily, knowing that if something went wrong during the coronation, it hadn't been my fault.

They never chose me.

I was born on the feast of the Immaculate Conception, that is, on the 8th of December. My father named me after the Immaculate Conception of the Virgin Mary, free from inherited sin thanks to her son Jesus. Evidently, he wished I had also been conceived immaculately, although I'm not sure that works in reverse. I cannot, till today, understand how I could possibly have been conceived at all, because with a father like mine, a consummate coward and prude, it was perfectly plausible that I had been incarnated in my mother's womb without any of his input. He was exactly like St Joseph, to be sure.

For years — and maybe I still believe this — I suspected that my parents had had sex only once, to make me, and since he was lucky enough to strike the first time, my father could put his mind at rest once and for all that he'd done his duty in the eyes of the Church, and that he could stop worrying about the business of consummating his marriage and creating his progeny. On my birthday he would always omit to tell me of my mother's shrieks as she spat me out into the world. Naturally, my father was at work on the day of my birth and not at my mother's bedside, gasping for breath and counting, and so he'd escaped the screams of her birth pangs lightly. Instead, he'd tell me that when Mary was conceived, she was exempt from all sin; that thanks to her son Jesus, who she would give birth to later, she had been born free from all sin, even inherited sin – especially inherited sin – and so, Mary didn't need a baptism.

I admit, I used to adore this story whenever he narrated it while rocking me back and forth in his lap, even though I was never sure who the baby belonged to, and who the mother was in this tale. They baptised me the very day I was born, just in case I didn't make it through the first night and fate would land me in limbo.

I never forgave them, of course. Not my father. Not the nuns. Not even the superiors of our catechism classes.

This young Nathaline writes down words and thoughts of such sweetness to me. Yesterday, I thought to tell her that in Malta, her name is more common among men than women. She immediately scribbled down that *we need to take back words from men, once and for all*. I didn't get what she meant by this, but I find her endearing, even if I don't always understand her.

On a different occasion she wrote to me that *words hurt only when they strike a chord in a person*. I asked her to elaborate.

When they hit the target, perhaps, rather than strike a chord, she wrote back.

"But my darling," I told her, "what are you trying to say?" Explain, enlighten me. And somehow she revealed to me that the written word, or indeed the spoken word, although it has the power to strike you down and kill you, isn't like a bullet. When you fire a bullet at someone and miss, you could easily hit and injure someone else instead, regardless of who they might be.

Words, she wrote, *wound only when they strike the intended target. No one else*.

"I don't know," I replied, "harsh words always seem to harm me, whether or not they were intended for me."

She wrote that she thought I had a point, because kind words can lift the spirit, no matter who they were meant for. And she continued telling me that since she arrived at the house, she's been writing a long letter of sorts to an important person in her life, and that she wasn't sure if she'd send it to them or not, so long as she was writing it, and that she was doing it for herself. However, she added, *I'd like you to read it, even though it's not meant for you*. It was as though she wanted to confirm everything we'd just been discussing, to resolve whether her words would hit me like a cannon shot.

I read about the Maltese sunshine, about her arrival here with us. In her writing I read about myself and was surprised by how, in her eyes, I appeared like one of the catechism superiors of my day. Then I read about the narrow streets of the town where she grew up, about the churches and the buildings, about the shops, the words, the silence. I got to know about the languages they speak over there, about her workplace, about the books, the warrior women, the thinkers and writers she liked to read about, and the strength their actions or their words filled her with, writers I don't know I've ever read before. And then about the tigers, how I laughed reading about these. I thought they were real tigers. *No*, she wrote, *they're extinct*, and I laughed even harder. It's unusual for me to laugh so much. And yet the young girl kept her composure and explained that her tigers were soldiers, subversive, ready to break away from their roots. To create a whole new society they were fighting to detach from the idea of equality with men entirely.

Roused by her words, I carried on reading. I wished that I too, in my old age, could bare my teeth, lash out and tear things apart until the blood was running down my chin. I gobbled down her scrawlings about today's women as though I didn't recognise them. I felt like I'd got stuck somewhere in the past, and then I was struck by a thought that left me cold. It occurred to me that I had taken shelter in this house and so remained oblivious to the changes happening on the outside. I shuddered at the sudden realisation that it was probably too late now. But it was as if Nathaline had read my mind: she smiled and scribbled down that *it was never too late to join the fight*.

When I encountered the details about the woman she was writing this missive for, I was thrown. Honestly, my blood froze and I began to shake all over on discovering that this composition I was reading was no less than a love letter, that Nathaline had a lover — how could I have guessed it? She had never mentioned it, never intimated anything to me about her. I still didn't know her name, whoever she was. I got so flustered, so utterly thrown off balance reading about their love, a wholesome and pure love between two young women, it made me tremble without quite knowing why. What was this now — was it agitation, confusion, fear? I began to picture them, Nathaline and her lover, laughing together in my mind, harmoniously holding hands, not uttering a single word to one another because there was no need for words, understanding passed easily between them without a shade of misapprehension, doubt, wickedness, fear or torment, and the world around them let them be.

I'm certain that I've witnessed these tableaux somewhere before, in my mind – definitely in my mind, because these were extraordinary scenes in reality. I know I had wished them, dreamed of them, desired them, and wanted, oh so badly, to be able to take her hand in mine, press her to me, to embrace her, kiss her, profess my love for her without fear that she'd recoil away from me or laugh at me, distance herself and join forces with everyone who was ever against us, and finally realise that they were right. I never forgot these scenes, despite doing everything I could to suppress them, to keep them at a distance.

Who? wrote Nathaline.

She wore a worried look on her face because she had never seen me this riled up. I lifted my palms up to my face to hide it — I didn't want to answer her, I didn't want to say her name. But Nathalie took my hands into hers and lowered them slowly, uncovering my face. She looked at me and I swear I saw her mouth the question, *who?* She couldn't have written it down, she was still holding my hands.

"Who?" she asked again, while holding my gaze, until I looked away and confessed:

"Dolor. It's always been Dolor."

And I lowered my head slowly into Nathaline's lap and exploded into tears. I sobbed and sobbed, and Nathaline comforted me until I had calmed down and, finally, rested.

IMMACOLATA CONCETTA

LORANNE VELLA | AUTHOR REFLECTION

Immacolata Concetta is an excerpt from the second section of the novel Marta Marta, titled "Immacolata Concetta". Marta Marta is a novel about gender oppression, told in five voices. Maria Dolores and Immacolata Concetta, the 80-year-old owners of the House of Pleasure, assume the roles of Mothers to the young women who live there too. Damjan, the third voice, fluidly transitions from one gender to another, from the self-isolating Damjan to Jeanne, who harbors an ambition to become the next girl to crown the Virgin during the 1st of May ritual. Through the feminist Nathaline, who is mute, we learn about the different waves of feminist activism in Belgium and France, and their complete absence in conservative Malta. The fifth voice belongs to the 400 year old house itself. Through Nathaline, she understands that the time has come for her windows and doors to shatter wide open to reveal what's inside to the outside world. Marta Marta is an experimental novel in Maltese which symbolically addresses key themes and preoccupations of current Maltese life, providing the groundwork for political and cultural discussion that enriches the discourse in Malta on topics such as abortion, feminism, gender identity and the prevalence of Catholic hegemony. The novel threads the line between the disorienting and the familiar, ensuring uniqueness and surprise while never devolving into obscurity. It is a mythological space in which contemporary Maltese mores are allowed to take root and submit themselves for dissection and exploration.

Marta Marta was published by Ede Books in 2022 and won the Malta National Book Prize in 2023.

IMMACOLATA CONCETTA

LORANNE VELLA

ORIGINAL MALTESE VERSION OF AN EXCERPT FROM "MARTA MARTA"

KLIEM BENEDITTA ġegħelni naħseb fl-imgħoddi, it-tifkiriet ngħożżhom daqskemm semmietli li tgħożżhom hi, iżda ma nħossx li qed jaħarbuli. U iva, xi dettalji nkun insejthom, oħrajn inkun żidthom biex inkompli nżewwaqhom jien. Mur ara x'differenza se tagħmel jekk id-dvalja dakinhar tal-ikla tal-festa għand in-nanna meta kelli disa' snin kinitx tassew bajda kif kont bqajt niftakarha jew le, u jekk le mela anki li n-nanna d-dvalja kienet tgħalliha fil-misħun imħallat bis-soder biex iġġibha bajda kont żidt jien biex nispjega l-bjuda tagħha f'moħħi. Fejn naf, ma nara li hemm xejn ħażin li tinsiehom it-tifkiriet kultant, sakemm ma tħarisx f'moħħok biex tfittixhom u tilmaħ il-vojt. Forsi hekk kienet qed tipprova tgħidli Beneditta, li bdiet tilmaħ il-vojt, li bil-kontra tiegħi, ma tafx terġa' timlieh malajr b'ħaġ'oħra. U ngħiduha kif inhi, anki jien nista' nifhem li jekk tħares 'il ġewwa u ssib il-vojt fejn kont qed tistenna li ssib il-mimli mhu gost għal ħadd. Jien mhux talli ma narax vojt jekk inħares lura warajja imma talli nsib tilja waħda nobis. Din fakkritni fil-mixi b'lura ta' Carmelina. Hekk ukoll missni għedtilha tagħmel lil Beneditta, lil kollha kemm huma jmissni nħeġġigħom iduru u jimxu bil-kontra. Xi waħda minn dawn għad jarawni għaddejja b'lura tul il-kuritur, imma lili mhux se jsejħuli granċ, tarax! Nafha sew jien it-triq li ħadt biex wasalt hawn, it-triq li terraqna flimkien jien u Dolor, m'għandi l-ebda vojt fejn jidħlu l-argumenti li ma jwasslu mkien ma' missieri minn meta għallimt lili nnifsi naqra sew kitbiet l-għorrief irġiel li jaf bihom kulħadd u anki dawk l-għorrief nisa li l-istorja minn dejjem inqas ħanina magħhom, u beda dieħel ftit melħ f'moħħi u bdejt naħsibha mod ieħor dwar kollox minn kif jaħsibha hu sal-aħħar jum nett qabel miet, ibda mill-ġenna u l-infern, Adam u Eva, id-dnub mejjet, id-dnub venjali, il-kmandamenti, is-sagramenti, u dwar kull twemmin li jemmen fih hu. Dwar xejn minn dan ma stajna naqblu, bqajna sal-aħħar niġġilduha dil-ġlieda li ma jista' jirbaħha ħadd. Għax missieri kellu moħħ magħluq li kien sakkru b'mitt elf katnazz u biex tgħaxxaq kien ta' rasu wkoll, daqskemm kont jien, jekk mhux iżjed. Avolja moħħi ridt niftħu beraħ u għal kull domma li kien jitfagħli kont noħroġ b'mitt mistoqsija, u hu kien iweġibni li lanqas mistoqsija waħda ma kien hemm bżonn, il-fidi hi fidi, temmen u ma tistaqsix. Naħlef li xħin ħa l-aħħar nifs ħadt ir-ruħ, imma għadni sa llum nhewden: tgħid kien ħadha fl-aħħar ir-risposta li m'hemmx ġenna tistennieh? Missieri miet iżda l-moħħ magħluq li ma jafx jaħseb mod ieħor sibnieh kullimkien madwarna, joħnoq u jaħsad kull ħsieb mod ieħor malli jinbet. Għedtilha, niftakarni, lil Dolor, qed nifga, qaltli issa naqilbuha ta' taħt fuq did-dinja. Għedtilha iva, naqilbuha, imma kif? Għall-ġlied ma ninqalax, lanqas kont se nkampa ħames minuti waqtha l-battalja. Folla rrabjata kontrija twaħħaxni, inbul taħti u nħalliha tiġi għalija, tgħaffiġni f'ħakka t'għajn. Le, m'iniex it-tip li nibdel id-dinja u naqlibha kollha ta' taħt fuq, mur ara kemm nista' nibdel jien, m'għandi saħħa ta' xejn, nispiċċa nkisser rasi ma' ħajt taż-żonqor minflok, nitfarrak jien u ma nkun bdilt xejn. Għedtilha 'l Dolor, le, il-ġlieda tiegħi mhux hekk, iżda taħsibx li beżgħana u se noqgħod għal li jgħiduli. Jekk il-kobor kbir wisq biex negħlbuh, mela nibda biex negħleb iż-żgħir, xi darba għad nasal. Jien kapaċi noħloq dinja żgħira għalija nnifsi minn dak kollu li jogħġobni madwari u nagħtih tifsira ġdida kif jaqbel lili, naf nisraq minn kollox kulma jgħodd għalija u narmi minnu dak kollu li ma jdoqqlix. Naf nadatta jien, għal ta' madwari, u mela ma nafx, imma jekk tħares sewwa tara li lil ta' madwari nkun addattajtu jien għalija fil-fatt. Fiċ-ċokon, kollox fiċ-ċokon nipprova nagħmel jien, għax fid-dinja jekk tara kbir wisq, qatt ma tasal, aħjar tara żgħir u twettaqhom l-affarijiet, milli toħlomhom biss u tibqa' fejn kont, jien hekk qaddisi, avolja jien il-ħolm qatt ma ngħidlu le, imma ħalliha, dik ħaġ'oħra. Qaltli Dolor, ħalli f'idi, int kisser u biddel fiċ-ċokon, il-kobor se naqilbu ta' taħt fuq jien. Qalbiena tassew din Dolor. Għadni niftakar kif dehret f'għajnejja hi u tgħidli dal-kelmiet, stħajjilt id-dija ħierġa minn wara rasha, għedtilha qisek dehra tal-Madonna. Qaltli liema waħda? Weġibtha, inti s-Sultana tal-Anġli. Infaqgħet tidħaq u staqsietni, meta se tqegħedhieli l-kuruna fuq rasi?

Qtajtha. Dis-sena għall-inkurunazzjoni tal-Madonna liż-żgħira l-ġdida Nathaline rrid. Kont qed insemmilha, dal-aħħar, li hemm min jemmen li l-Madonna ħarġet tqila b'Ġesù minn widintha, u Nathaline tatni ħarsa bħal donnha ma fehmitx. Fissirtilha li tant ma kinitx tinżlilhom lil ċerti għorrief irġiel tal-Knisja jimmaġinawha, lill-Verġni Marija, tittaqqal billi tintmiss bejn saqajha, bħalma toħroġ tqila kwalunkwe mara oħra, li dehrilhom li omm Alla ntebħet b'Ġesù f'ġufha hekk kif semgħet kliem l-Anġlu jitħabbrilha f'widintha. Żergħalha ż-żerriegħa f'widintha, għedtilha, imma ma nafx f'liema waħda, hux tal-lemin jew tax-xellug. Iż-żerriegħa tista' tkun in-nifs tal-Anġlu, u tista' tkun il-kelma, spjegajtilha, għax naf kemm tħobbu Nathaline l-kliem. Għalhekk il-Kelma saret bniedem, għax waqgħet fuq widnet Marija. Nathaline qagħdet kwieta, stħajjiltha qed tomgħodhom waħda waħda l-kelmiet li kont għedtilha, ħassejtni dak il-ħin jien stess kont l-Anġlu li fesfistilha f'widintha din l-aħbar u hi l-Madonna qed tintebaħ bit-tifsira ta' li kont qed ngħidilha. Iva, minn dakinhar għadni ma waqaftx naħseb f'Nathaline bl-ilbies abjad u l-mant ċelesti, bid-dijadema f'idejha miexja fuq quddiem tal-purċissjoni, b'rasha baxxuta, lejn l-istatwa tal-Verġni Mqaddsa li għandna fil-bitħa. Dik it-tifla wiċċ il-Madonna għandha, mal-ewwel lemħa li kelli tagħha ntbaħt, stajt naraha bil-mant fuq rasha, jinkwadralha wiċċha, ħsibtha l-inkarnazzjoni vera u proprja tax-xbieha ta' Marija Santissima. Lil Dolor għadni m'għedtilha b'xejn minn dan, imma Dolor għal dil-festa dejjem tħalli f'idi, taf li għalija pjaċir.

Fl-ewwel ta' Mejju l-iskola konna nħejju festa kbira, kont inkun ilni nistennieha mis-sena ta' qabel, tant kien ikollna eċitament fuqna aħna t-tfajliet. Is-sorijiet ta' San Ġużepp, fejn kont skola, kienu jistiednu kemm lilna l-bniet, libsin kollha bl-abjad u b'qoffa ċkejkna mimlija fjuri f'idejna, kif ukoll 'il-ġenituri tagħna, għall-inkurunazzjoni tal-Madonna. L-isbaħ tfajla fostna dik is-sena kienet tintgħażel biex tqiegħed il-kuruna fuq ras l-istatwa, statwa kbira kienet tkun, ngħidlek jien kienet ikbar mit-tfajla li kienet titla' fuq is-sellum maġenbha biex tqegħdilha l-kuruna fuq rasha. Niftakarha sew il-kuruna, fuq l-imħadda kwadra tal-bellus ikħal lewn is-sema fir-rebbiegħa, f'idejn it-tfajla hi u tmexxi l-purċissjoni. Kont inkun imwerwra li xi ħaġa tmur ħażin u tiżżerżqilha minn fuq l-imħadda jew minn fuq ras il-Madonna. Ma stajtx niddeċiedi jekk kontx nifraħ jew le kieku s-sena ta' wara kellhom jagħżlu lili biex ninkurunaha. Kont nifraħ, żgur mhux forsi, mhux talli hekk, talli kont nixtieq fuq li nixtieq li xi darba jmiss lili mmexxi l-purċissjoni tat-tfajliet lejn il-Madonna, jien fuq quddiem bil-kuruna u t-tfajliet warajja bil-qfief mimlija petali mfewħin. Fl-istess ħin il-biża' li l-kuruna tiżżerżaqli minn idi u nfotti festa sħiħa kien iwaħħaxni u kont ngħid le, le, aħjar jekk ma jagħżlunix. Għax bilqiegħda fuq is-siġġu mat-tfajliet l-oħra kollha fil-bitħa tal-iskola tas-sorijiet, bil-ktejjeb tal-innijiet f'idejja, inkanta l-innu ta' Sidtna ta' Lourdes, l-Angelus, is-Sultana tal-Anġli, l-Ave Marija, is-Sliem Għalik Marija, inti d-dawl, il-Kewkba ta' Filgħodu u l-Omm Ħanina, għallimna l-għaqal, għallimna l-imħabba, jien u nosserva r-ritwal tal-inkurunazzjoni kollu kemm hu mill-platea, u nitlob lil Sidtna u 'l Ommna li nagħti lili nnifsi lilha u b'turija ta' devozzjoni, noffri għajnejja, widnejja, ħalqi, qalbi u kollni kemm jien lilha mingħajr ma nżomm lura u xejn għalija. Jien nintelaq kollni kemm jien f'idejha, biex tħarisni, hekk biss stajt nieħu nifs aħjar għax kont naf li jekk xi ħaġa tmur ħażin waqt it-tqegħid tal-kuruna ma kienx ikun tort tiegħi.

Qatt ma ntgħażilt.

Twelidt nhar il-Kunċizzjoni, voldieri fit-tmienja ta' Diċembru, u missieri semmieni għall-Immakulata Kunċizzjoni tal-Verġni Marija, ħielsa mid-dnub tan-nisel bis-saħħa ta' binha Ġesù, sforz kemm xtaq li anki jien ġejt konċepita immakulata, ma nafx jekk taħdimx b'lura. Għadni s'issa ma nistax nifhem kif qatt stajt ġejt ikkonċepita jien, għax b'missier bħal missieri, beżżiegħ mid-dublett u ta' taħtu li ma ngħidlekx, wieħed anki jista' jibda jemmen li fil-każ tiegħi ġejt inkarnata f'ġuf ommi mingħajr ma ħa kedda l-missier. Bħal San Ġużepp biex niftiehmu. Għal snin shaħ, u forsi hekk għadni, kelli s-suspett li missieri u ommi kellhom x'jaqsmu darba biss, biex għamlu lili, u billi b'xorti tajba mill-ewwel ċaqqamha, missieri seta' jserraħ rasu darba għal dejjem li f'għajnejn il-Knisja kien għamel dmiru u seta' anki jieqaf iħabbel rasu dwar dil-biċċa xogħol tal-ikkunsmar taż-żwieġ u t-tnissil tal-ulied. F'għeluq snini kien dejjem jirrakkuntali mhux dwar it-twerżiq li werżqet ommi biex beżqitni f'did-dinja. Sintendi, dakinhar li twelidt jien missieri x-xogħol kien, u mhux jonfoħ u jgħodd maġenb is-sodda t'ommi, u allura t-twerżiq tal-ħlas ħelsu ħafif ħafif. Kien jirrakkuntali, minflok, li meta ġiet konċepita Marija, ma kien daħal fiha l-ebda dnub, li bil-mertu ta' Ġesù li kien se jitwildilha iktar 'il quddiem, ommu bħala tarbija kienet twieldet safja minn kull dnub, anki dak tan-nisel, speċjalment dak tan-nisel, u allura Marija ma kellhiex bżonn magħmudija biex tinħeles minn dad-dnub. Nammetti li din l-istorja kont nogħxa warajha meta kien jgħidhieli huwa u jbandalni fuq ħoġru, minkejja li ma kontx nista' naqbad art ta' min kienet it-tarbija u min kienet l-omm f'dar-rakkont. Għammduni dakinhar stess li twelidt, li ma mmurx ma nwassalx sal-għada u nispiċċalu l-limbu.

Sintendi, qatt ma ħfirtilhom. La 'l missieri. La lis-sorijiet. U lanqas lis-Superjuri tal-Mużew.

Kemm tiktibli kelmiet u ħsibijiet sbieħ diż-żgħira Nathaline. Ilbieraħ fettilli ngħidilha li f'Malta isimha iktar nużawh għall-irġiel milli għan-nisa. Kitbitli fil-pront li l-kelma rridu nisirquha darba għal dejjem mingħand ir-raġel. Ma fhimtx x'riedet tgħid biha, niggustaha xorta avolja ma nifhimhiex. Darb'oħra kitbitli li l-kliem iweġġa' biss meta jolqot il-likk, għedtilha spjegali ftit ieħor għax ridt nifhimha sew din tal-kelma u l-likk. Kitbitli li forsi tir aħjar minn likk. Għedtilha, imma ruħi dwar xiex qed tgħidli? Fissirli daqsxejn ħalli nifhem. U minn hawn u minn hemm fehmitni li l-kelma miktuba, jew dik mitkellma, avolja għandha s-saħħa li tidrob u toqtol, mhijiex bħal balla li jekk tisparaha lil xi ħadd u ma tolqtux tista' tolqot u tidrob li xi ħaddieħor minflok, ikun min ikun. Kitbitli li kelma tweġġa' biss meta tolqot lil dak li hi maħsuba u miktuba għalih u lil ħadd iktar ħliefu. Għedtilha, ma nafx jien, il-kliem iebes minn ħaddieħor dejjem donnu jweġġagħni, ikun għalija jew ma jkunx. Imbagħad tbissmitli u kitbitli li forsi għandi raġun, għax il-kliem sabiħ jaf iferraħ ikun għal min ikun. U kompliet tgħidli li kemm ilha hawn qed tikteb bħal ittra twila lil persuna importanti f'ħajjitha, lanqas biss ċerta hix se tibgħatha jew le, l-aqwa li qed tiktibha u li qed tiktibha għaliha. Iżda, kompliet, nixtieqek taqraha int avolja mhux miktuba għalik. Bħal donnha riedet tara jekk hux minnu dak li konna għadna kif tħaddittna dwaru, biex taqtagħha jekk kliemha kienx se jkollu effett bħal balla ta' kanun fuqi jew le.

Qrajt dwar ix-xemx Maltija, dwar il-wasla tagħha għandna, f'kitbietha qrajt dwari stess u stagħġibt kif f'għajnejha dhertilha bħal waħda mis-Superjuri ta' dari. Imbagħad qrajt dwar it-toroq dojoq tal-belt fejn trabbiet, dwar il-knejjes u l-bini, dwar il-ħwienet, dwar il-kliem, dwar is-skiet. Sirt naf dwar il-lingwi t'hemmhekk, dwar fejn kienet taħdem, dwar il-kotba, dwar in-nisa ġellieda, ħassieba u kittieba li taqra dwarhom, dwar is-saħħa li ħadet minn għemilhom jew minn kliemhom, kittieba bħal dawn ma nafnix li qatt qrajt. Imbagħad dwar it-tigri, kemm dħaqt naqra dwarhom dawn, ħsibthom ta' veru, qaltli le, dawk estinti, u iktar dħaqt. Mhux soltu tiegħi nidħaq hekk jien. Iżda ċ-ċkejkna baqgħet serja u kitbitli li t-tigri tagħha ġellieda, sovversivi, lesti jqaċċtu mill-għeruq, għal soċjetà għalkollox ġdida qed jiġġieldu lil hinn mill-ugwaljanza mal-irġiel. Komplejt naqra, ħassejt kliemha jqanqalni, xtaqt

97

jien ukoll fi xjuħiti nikxef snieni, nigdem u nbiċċer bid-demm iċarċar ma' geddumi. Qrajt bil-qalb kitbietha dwar in-nisa tal-lum bħal donni lanqas għarafthom. Ħassejtni kont weħilt żmien ilu xi mkien, għaddieli minn rasi ħsieb li kexkixni, stħajjilt li kont ingħalaqt f'did-dar għall-kenn u qatt ma ntbaħt bil-bidliet li seħħew fuq barra. Dehxa tul dahri nebbħitni li issa kien forsi tard wisq. Iżda Nathaline donnha qratli moħħi, tbissmitli u kitbitli li qatt mhu tard wisq biex tidħol għalih dal-ġlied. Iżda l-iktar li nfxilt meta qrajt dwar dik li għaliha kitbitu dan kollu, u naħlef li ġismi kesaħ bid-dehxa qawwija li issa qabditni tul ġismi kollu kemm hu xħin intbaħt li din mhijiex ħlief ittra ta' mħabba għal maħbubitha, li Nathaline għandha maħbuba, fejn qatt kont bsartha din? Qatt ma kienet semmietha, qatt ma tarrfitli xejn dwarha. Lanqas minn kitbietha ma għadni fhimt x'jisimha, min hi. Naħlef li tħawwadt fuq li tħawwadt, naqra dwar imħabbithom, imħabba safja u pura bejn żewġ tfajliet, inħossni nirtogħod imma ma nafx eżatt għaliex. X'inhija din tiegħi, issa, x'inhu dan, taħwid, tfixkil, biża'? Sirt narahom lil Nathaline u l-maħbuba, jidħqu flimkien narahom f'moħħi, id f'id għalenija, ma jgħidu xejn waħda lill-oħra, m'hemmx għalfejn, kollox jinftiehem bejniethom, m'hemmx ħaġa mifhuma b'oħra, m'hemmx dubju, m'hemmx ħażen, la biżgħat, la turment, bejniethom jiftiehmu bla kliem, u d-dinja madwarhom tħallihom bi kwiethom, naħlef dawn ix-xeni ġa rajthom qabel xi mkien, f'moħħi, dejjem f'moħħi għax barra minn moħħi kienu xeni ta' barra minn hawn, naf li xtaqthom, ħlomthom, ridthom, ridt u kif li nkun nista' naqbdilha idha f'idi, nagħfasha miegħi, inħaddanha, inbusha, ngħidilha bi mħabbti lejha mingħajr il-biża' li tinġibed minni u tidħaq bija, li titbiegħed minni u tingħaqad, minflok, ma' kull min minn dejjem kien kontrina u issa tifhem kemm kellhom raġun. Dawn xeni li ma nsejt qatt, afli kollox għamilt biex inbegħedhom minni, nitbiegħed minnhom. Kitbitli Nathaline, min? Fuq wiċċha kellha ħarsa inkwetata għax qatt ma kienet ratni mbaqbqa daqshekk. Għattejt wiċċi bil-pali ta' jdejja, ma ridtx inweġibha, ma ridtx inlissen lsimha, imma Nathaline qabditli jdejja f'idejha u niżżlithomli minn quddiem għajnejja bil-mod, ħarset lejja u naħlef li lissnitha l-kelma min? Ma setgħetx kitbithieli, idejha kienu maqbudin ma' tiegħi. *Min?* reġgħet staqsietni, u baqgħet tħares fiss f'għajnejja sa ma baxxejt ħarsti u għedtilha Dolor, minn dejjem Dolor, u niżżilt rasi bil-mod sa ma middejtha fuq ħoġor Nathaline u bkejt bikja twila nolfoq waħda f'waħda u Nathaline bennitni sa ma kkalmajt u ħassejtni nistrieħ.

TALE OF A GRASSHOPPER AND A TOMATO

LOUIS BRIFFA

TRANSLATED BY ROSE MARIE CARUANA

1

To glean your goodness, fruit, each single day
Grasshopper savours himself in wonder
and maybe for a little while discerns
what being an insect truly means:
all juice and flesh –
I risk my sap and sinews all
betwixt the squeeze of tiny fingers
that a naughty boy
keeps hold.

For you I must forego
my jumps and starts to reach up high
for here I can neither rise,
nor carefully descend.
To break my fall should I collapse
I find no silken dome
billowing joyfully
in a summer breeze
but the slippery frost
of a polished prison.
I forgot
for your sake
the dense delicious web of love
on which, with my beloved,
long hours did I spend asleep
until the kindled magic would die down
and steal away I would
beneath a layer of dark green
to once again shamelessly pulsate,
in secret
with another.

Each time you are manhandled from up high 2
by the tender fingers
of that kind-hearted lad,
I see the light come kiss your oval flesh
and the shadow of your shining flanks
Settle a cool mantle
Over me.

When bounteous by me you suddenly fall 3
but smears of scarlet splodges do I see.
And yet bloodstains ... what are bloodstains,
if not you, a throbbing creature,
enveloping me in scent and colour,
since nothing else for me exists?

The hungry savage snap can fatal prove
and turns you into easy prey.
But seemingly, no, for you're nothing else
but an honest creature -
A faithful fount awash with life in bloom!

In moist and yielding pulp I'm lost o fruit.

The juice you leak acidic proves to be,
suffusing me with vengeance through
time-flakes of fury endured all alone.

4

O bundle of vegetable substances
that turned my flesh to copper
and my mandibles
to sensual red rods:
can you feel them?
The time will come when they'll latch on to you
and I'll ravish you
callously
time without count.

How robust and agile I am ...

With skilful pleasure
through the eye's thin veil
you'll see me mount you,
part you,
aflame with gusts
that rouse your flesh.

I'm bathed in sweat each time that we make love
and all my rage dissolves to tiny flowers
around myself, around the husk that's all
that's left
around a swirl of seeds
that had the taste of rust and were spat out.

Perceive the crimson tail-end of this yarn   5
where two are panting,
juices flowing...
But not in an atmosphere
with pretence of procreation
reduced
to stem's slight thrusting up and thrusting down...

This forced marriage,
believe you me,
can only comprehended be
by a grasshopper and a tomato.

The title I gave this poem, The Tale of a Grasshopper and a Tomato ironically and figuratively centres on a sexual relationship between an insect and a fruit. The subject, of course, is metaphorical, almost cynically highlighting a forced romp in a run-of-the-mill sexual experience. The poem actually evolved from a recent very deep reflection of mine, which forced me to hit mercilessly at a society that has thrown consensual love and affection to the wind. It also hits darkly and sadly at male superiority and domination over the female species during the primordial quest for love, respect and devotion, with even darker undertones when love is actually marred and abused by physical violence and, very often. at times, even by rape and utter humiliation.

L-ISTORJA TA' ĠURAT U TA' TADAMA

LOUIS BRIFFA

ORIGINAL MALTESE VERSION OF "THE GRASSHOPPER AND THE TOMATO"

Biex niekol minnek, frotta, ta' kuljum –   **1**
ġurat intiegħem b'għoġba lili nnifsi
u forsi għal ftit nifhem
xi tfisser tkun insett: meraq u laħam –
nissogra merqti u ftieti
fis-swaba' ċkejkunija
ta' sabi b'kopp daqsiex.

Għalik kelli nastjieni
mill-qbiż u mit-titjir fuqani
għax hawn ma nistax nogħla,
jo nkun preċiż fi nżuli.
Tilqagħni jekk niġġarraf
mhux koppla tal-ħarir
tintefaħ bi pjaċir
mir-rjieħ sajfija
'mma l-kesħa żelliqija
ta' magħluq illustrat.

Insejt
għalik
l-għanqbuta sfiqa u ħelwa tan-namur
li fuqha, mal-maħbuba,
kont norqod sigħat twal
sakemm tintfielna l-waħma tal-maġija
u b'serqa niżgiċċalha
taħt mitraħ aħdar skur
u vili nerġa' nserser
bil-ħabi
lil ħaddieħor.

Kuldarba li jerħuk kemxejn mill-għoli 2
is-swaba' rotob baqta
tat-tfajjel ġeneruż,
id-dawl narah ibus ġismek żenguli
u dell ġenbejk leqqija
inħossu bħal liżar ta' frisk
għal fuqi.

Kif b'sabta taqa' ħdejja bħal matmura
ħlief ċapep ħmura mżellġa ma narax.

'Mma d-dmija... x'inhi d-dmija,
'kk mhux int, j'anima tbaqbaq,
li troddli lewn u riħa
għax ħliefek ma nagħrafx?

Fi priża faċli ndonnok... 3

'Mma donnok, le, m'intix
ħlief ħlejqa ħorra.

Aċtuż l-ilma li terħi.
Jimlieni bil-vendetta
fil-furja tal-mumenti mġarrba waħdi.

Ja sorra ta' sustanzi veġetali **4**
li bdiltli ġismi f'ramm
u fildiferru aħmar
senswali l-palpi:
tħosshom?
Għad bihom niggranfak
u nabbużak
bla kont
u skruplu.

Robust u aġli jien...

Bis-sengħa tal-pjaċir
u l-velu rqiq tal-ħabba
tarani nirkbek,
naqsmek
f'buffuri ta' nirien
li jonfoħ laħmek.

Nixxarrab għasra jien kulmeta nħobbok
u ddubli r-rabja fi fjur żgħir madwari
mal-qoxra li biss
tibqa'
ma' ħemel ta' żerriegħa
bit-togħma tas-sadid mibżuqa barra.

Tifhmuh id-denb hamrani tal-istorja   5
bejn tnejn jilehġu,
joqtru...
fi globu ħġieġ –
il-mikrokożmu ta' Ħolqien
irejjaħ u żellieġ.

Daż-żwieġ sfurzat
emmnuni
jifhmuh biss
tadama u ġurat.

WOMBS ON STRIKE

KRISTINA BORG

Shh! Shh! Shhhhhh!
Easy… bil-mod, mara, bil-mod, calm down
Tarax kbir, tarax iżżejjed, think twice, plan ahead
Lower your sights – Shh! Shh! Shhhhhh!

When are you having children? Meta se tbennen?
Le – Għax le? If you can, why wouldn't you?
Għax le – How dare you? Ma tistħix?
Għax le! – Don't worry, you'll change your mind. La tikber,
taraha differenti, your attitude will change – Għax le?

La tikber. Imma torqodx
Before it's too late – we freeze your eggs?
Try again. Push, push, harder!
Ippruvajt biżżejjed? Push, push, harder! Push, -ush, shh, shhhh! … push to adopt
Ma tridx tadotta? Die alone, you

self-centred, selfish bitch
Condemned to teenage crudeness – unripe, heartless responsibility
Bla tfal, bla responsabbiltà, tiżvoga fix-xogħol
Jew tibża', courageless, something's wrong with you, you
horrible person, the reason of evil

Failure of humanity, falluta
On your breasts, the brand of shame

On my breasts, your brand of shame, I wear a scarlet letter
Scarlet 'A' – aħmar qawwi, penetranti, skarlat

I wear a scarlet letter
    as I work extra hours till late, justify my leave, nibq' hemm, nibq' għaddejja
    as I choose not to make it to the motherhood pedestal,
    nonmotherhood, crucified for not following the preordained path.

Scarlet 'A'
    as you make me doubt what it could have been like,
    you decide for me, choose for me, parent me.
    How are you more grown up than I am?
    Jien min jien? Who is the real me? The me perceived by all?

Aħmar skarlat inxidd
    waqt li naqdef kontra l-kurrent, itektek,
    l-arloġġ itektek -tek-tek -tek-tek.
    Ageing out the threshold, should I have or should I not?
    Doomed by boobs, what is not carried in my womb,
    the be-all and end-all of my existence.
    Clinically raped through IVF, fulfilling my human function,

I choose not to. Dragged, entrapped into a substitute,
a mother to – my paintings, my students, my books
a mother to – my pets, my juniors, my nephews and nieces.
A stupid, constant struggle
a struggle of self-contradiction.

But, hey what? What the fuck?
I shed away the scarlet letter, month after month
demmi jbaqbaq, jisplodi, idub u jċarċar.
The letter dissolves, melts, melts, melts -ts -ts -ts
gradually, painfully, silently, softly – steadily.

I'm free 'n' fly high
bil-ġwienaħ imberħa, I travel far and wide
life is fun, flexi – a childfree adventure.
Dreams unchained, inlaħħaq ma' xiex irrid – I'm Able,
almost equated to Mr fellow. I have Agency,
I pause to process, I pause to focus, progress -ss -ss -ss
Eureka! Allow me be my best,
hold space for myself, embrace myself

– an Adult in charge of my life, I choose
what my womb carries, carries, (un)carries, carries, (un)carries
I choose to deprogramme myself
unfollow the pattern, I seek other
family visions – ta' erbgħa, ta' tnejn, waħdi, x'jimporta? I refuse to romanticise.
What makes you more of a woman? Why am I less of a woman?
Why don't I have children? And you, and you,
you, you, why do you have children?
I choose my dream – selfish, somewhat?
You choose your dream – selfish, somewhat?

I don't have children, I don't want to – I don't, I won't.
Yes, I'm a mother to – my projects, my pets, my passion,
you call it mother; I call it love – love works,
bħal rummiena b'demmha jċarċar, juicy
prolific pomegranate, one idea
leads to another, fertile barrenness.
My life, my choice – conscious, with responsibility
The world is on fire! The future looks bleak,
Inħobbok, u ma nistax intik dak li ħaqqek, qas siġra?
Tfal m'għandix – m'għandix, ma rridx

Should I have or should I not?
My life, my choice – conscious, with responsibility
Why doubt? Why wonder?

My life, my choice,
My choice, my love,
My love, my life

Wombs on Strike* *(2024) is inspired by a series of conversations with women aged between 30-45 years old, and who have opted not to have children. Taking such a path, breaking the stereotype of women as mothers, has been described as a social stigma and considered a taboo subject. As one woman illustrated, such experience is akin to wearing a scarlet letter. Just like the rebellious, female protagonist of Nathaniel Hawthorne's 1850 novel The Scarlet Letter – who is accused and sentenced to wear a scarlet 'A', which in the story stands for adultery – the women who shared their experience of the no-child option also feel accused of being dishonourable and heartless, often denied agency rather than appreciated for their abilities. The work explores how this group of women take hold of the words used to shame their choice and shift such shame into resistance, opening up a discussion towards mainstreaming diverse life choices with the hope of embracing better equality.*

The submitted piece is bilingual (EN and MT). It originally developed as a multilingual (EN, MT and ES) poem which served as groundwork for a soundscape artistic project that was presented early 2024 in Malta and Barcelona, as part of an interdisciplinary exhibition that explores the diverse meanings and implications of the word 'māter'.

*in Chollet M. (2023). In Defence of Witches: Why Women Are Still on Trial. Picador, p.89.

IL-PLURAL TA' JIENA MHUX DEJJEM AĦNA
THE PLURAL OF "I" IS NOT ALWAYS "WE"

NADIA MIFSUD

tixxellef tara 'l-ħuttaf jitbiegħed
tħossha se tinqasam felli felli
tixtieq tista' tifrex ġwinħajha, ittir
hi ukoll mar-riħ qabel ma ssir baħħ
jew kamra ġo dar tistenna
ħa (terġa') tkennen — lil min?
m'hemmx li jistenbħu sura dat-toroq
m'hemmx li jdub dal-griż bħal imdendel
mis-sema. goff u sikkanti dal-griż — pariġġ
id-dħaħen jinbeżqu miċ-ċmieni u l-karozzi,
pariġġ il-bankini, pariġġ il-bini bla sura,
pariġġ ħsibijietha midruba. morri ħsibijietha.
morri iktar mill-kafè li ferrgħet bla ma
xorbot dalgħodu. f'ħalqha, it-togħma
pessma tal-ħolma li mbuttatha mis-sodda
qabel it-tħanxira tal-iżviljarin. ħolmot li
ntilfet, tfittex il-jinijiet tagħha. għax
mhux veru dak li kienu tambrulha
l-iskola. il-plural ta' jiena mhux dejjem
aħna. u jinijiet għandha ruxxmata. ibda
minn dik li ssawret ikkulurita f'għajnejn
nannitha, imbenna fi tbissimtha. jew dik
li ommha xebgħet tipprova ssewwi —
hi ġġarrab
ommha toftoq
iġġarrab
terġa' toftoq
terġa' ġġarrab.
tixraqlek.
u tkun se tixraq fid-dmugħ, tħares lejn
dik il-jien ixxewwek fil-mera. hemm bżonn
tolfoq, iwa? miniex nolfoq. tigdibx.

(qatt ma) drat tismagħha dik il-kelma —
tigdibx
tigdibx
tigdibx.
u allura nfexxet
tikteb
tikteb
tikteb
tħarref kemm tiflaħ
taqla' minn żniedha
bla ħadd qatt ma ssogra jgħidilha qed tigdeb.
(gidba: g-d-b
kitba: k-t-b
kemm tieqaf tleħħen il-konsonanti
u tiskot inti magħhom.
tħalli 'l-karta titkellem minflokok.)
imbagħad ... hu — il-ħrafa li ma kinitx
taf tafx tikteb. għalih żanżnet l-isbaħ jien
tagħha. u żifnu. lagħbu dawra durella, onġi
onġi onġella. imma meta ġew għan-noli,
ipprefera jibqa' moħbi, imgħannaq ma' rġulitu.
u hi żżardet tfittxu. fittxitu bla taf sewwasew
fejn kien barra u fejn kien ġewwa, sakemm
dalam, sakemm ftit ftit xejn ma baqa' —
'qas leħnu, 'qas l-ittri tal-sms, 'qas għajnejh
jgħumu fiċ-ċpar. xejn għajr sodda bierda,
u kikkra kafè morra minsija fuq il-bank
tal-kċina. u s-sigar tat-triq nofshom imneżżgħa,
inemmsulha. jitħassruha. u l-griż stinat,
bħal imdendel mis-sema. iteftef fiha. għoddu
nifidha. u ... taf. taf li, jekk trid, għadha tista'
tiggranfa mal-kuluri mbissma f'għajnejn nannitha.
taf li issa jeħtiġilha tfassal jiena oħra. jeħtiġilha
tiftakar kulma għallmitha ommha — il-kmiem,
il-kfief, il-ġmigħ, iċ-ċinta, l-inforra. kollox
għallmitha tħit ommha — anki qarsa.
fl-isem tal-omm u tal-bint u tad-demm li
jċarċar kull xahar. mur, qaltilha, u emmen.

THE FEMININE VOICE OF MALTA

Inside the Poet Mind: A Detailed Reflection by Nadia Mifusd

This text was initially written as part of a project that brought together nine contemporary voices, all female, from the Maltese poetry scene, many of whom are featured in this anthology — Clare Azzopardi, Miriam Calleja, Leanne Ellul, Claudia Gauci, Elizabeth Grech, Maria Grech Ganado, Simone Inguanez, Klara Vassallo, and myself.

The aim of this project was twofold. First and foremost, we wanted to pay homage to Maria Grech Ganado, Malta's first Poet Laureate and mentor-role-model to many women writers in Malta. But we also wanted to celebrate our diversity, the experiences and the quirks that shape our individuality. Intertextuality plays a prominent role in this poem. Not only are there explicit references to some of Grech Ganado's early poems, but the attentive reader will also spot several allusions to international writers, ranging from Maya Angelou to Nayirrah Waheed.

In this poem, I celebrate matrilineal ties and address underlying tensions in such relationships. Several elements in this text stem from my personal experience. I spent the first seven years of my life living with my parents at my maternal grandmother's house; I grew up with two nurturing but highly contrasting mother figures. As a mother of two daughters myself, I have become increasingly aware of all the intricacies that are passed down from one generation to the next, how we are shaped through the Other's gaze, how hurtful it can be to conform to that gaze and live up to another person's expectations. One of the central images in this poem is that of a mother constantly altering her daughter's ill-fitting clothes, until the latter can no longer relate to the image of herself that she sees in the mirror.

When writing in Maltese, I tend to opt for words that have more than one meaning. This central image is built around two such verbs: *'iġġarrab'*, which means *'to try on a piece of clothing'* but also *'to experience/endure something'* and *'tixraqlek'* (*'it suits you'*) versus *'tixraq'* (*'to choke on something'*). While the mother is content with the alterations, the daughter breaks down, unable to recognize herself any more. The real issue is not the ill-fitting garment, but the daughter's personality which the mother keeps unstitching and tacking over and over again.

The title of this poem, *Il-plural ta' jiena mhux dejjem aħna* translates as *The plural of I isn't always we* and refers to how we learn to accommodate people around us, how different facets of our personality rise to the surface/ remain concealed depending on who we are interacting with. Maybe I'm wrong, but I have always felt that this is something women are taught to do from an early age, to a larger degree than men. Thus, the female persona in this poem dons her finest self for her male lover (*'għalih żanżnet l-isbaħ jien tagħha'*) before the two of them engage in a strange dance which feels playful at first but eventually leaves her frayed (*'u hi żżardet tfittxu'*):

> [...] but when they played hide-and-seek,
> he chose to remain hidden, embracing his manhood.

This estranged lover ends up being 'the one story she wasn't sure she'd ever be able to write (*'hu — il-ħrafa li ma kinitx taf tafx tikteb'*). Writing is one of the ways in which the persona of this poem accommodates the world — it is a convenient disguise that replaces falsehood. In Maltese, the verbs *'writing'* (*'tikteb'*) and *'lying'* (*'tigdeb'*) are very close in terms of sound. The voiced 'g' and 'd' of 'tigdeb' are replaced by the unvoiced 'k' and 't' of *'tikteb'*. I have always been intrigued by this phonetic coincidence — the narratives and characters that are silently concocted by writers to express thoughts and emotions that may remain unvoiced in real life or perceived as unacceptable and perilous when voiced. For the persona of the poem, everything feels gray (*'griż'*) and bitter (*'morri ħsibijietha'*) in the aftermath of her loss, until she realizes how strong a legacy her ties with her mother and her grandmother are, how these two figures were in fact a repository of knowledge, a source of wisdom. She finds solace in the recollection of the *'colorful self'* her grandmother perceived in her as a child (*'[il-jiena] li ssawret ikkulurita f'għajnejn nannithu'*), and her mother's sewing becomes a powerful, invaluable life lesson rather than a mere skill:

> she knows she needs another patterned I. she needs to
> remember all that her mother taught her – sleeves,
> hems, gathering, waistbands, linings. her mother
> taught her how to sew everything – even darts.

A dart is '*qarsa*' in Maltese, but '*qarsa*' can also mean '*a pinch*', i.e. something that is painful. The poem ends on a riff on the Trinitarian formula that generally accompanies the sign of the cross. Instead of the usual '*In the name of the Father, and of the Son, and of the Holy Spirit. Amen*', the final two lines of the poem not only celebrate matrilineal ties but also highlight menstruation as a core element of women's unique, powerful legacy:

in the name of the mother and of the daughter and of the blood
that trickles each month. go, she said, and believe.

VJOLA BĦAX-XAĦXIEĦ

RITA SALIBA

Subgħajja jippruvaw jilqgħu
s-sirda nieżla bħal star iswed
fuq dirgħajja mikxufin,
jostru erba' qmura
mnaqqxa minn difrejk ġo laħmi;
marka oħra li ridt tħallili
biex turi li jien tiegħek.
Il-feriti qed jagħlqu
jħallu marki vjola bħax-xaħxieħ,
jidhru aktar kif jidħol staġun frisk
u tgħib minn ġildti s-smura tas-sajf.

Għedtli li posti f'rokna mudlama
fejn ma jħares lejja ħadd.
Imm'issa li qtajt dal-ktajjen
noħroġ għall-wens tal-lejl,
nilqa' d-dlam ...
li jsaħħaħni.

Sometimes life throws on your path a special woman, and as you get to know her, the mask she wears becomes transparent. She has worn, or still wears, the marks of domestic violence – especially the emotional scars that seem to penetrate the skin from within. I admire the courage of those who have persevered through abuse. Often, society does not help these silent victims. The stigma and taboo persist: She should have seen all this before! She knew what she was going in for! Comments like these annihilate her experiences and perpetuate her resistance to seek help. This poem, perhaps, is my feeble reaction to every tragedy that we read in the news, watch on our screens, and hear through the grapevine. The tragedy of each victim is society's collective tragedy. We are covering the wounds with a gauze, fooling ourselves that they would heal on their own...

Vjola bħax-xaħxieħ, *translated to English as* Purple Marks, *was written in my native language, Maltese. Not only does the Maltese language communicate my clearest, natural thoughts, the language is very direct, contrasting darkness and clarity. I write about tradition and rebellion; I write in the language I think and pray in; I write in the language that creates a direct line between myself and the reader. For that reason,* Vjola bħax-xaħxieħ *could be written in no other language.*

TIXTIEQ ITTIR

LARA CALLEJA

Ir-riħ kien forza sitta. Xagħar is-siġar f'dak l-għoli kien ried jitqaċċat minn zkuktu u jerħilha x'imkien ieħor. Is-sema ċara. U l-karozza wkoll għoddha riedet tinqata' minn mal-art għal preċipizzju ta' isfel. Idea eċċitanti u eżotika għal min m'għandux bajd jagħmilha. Għafset il clutch u ħallitha first, allijistajkun il-hand break mhux biżżejjed biex iżżomm il-karozza ankarata f'dak it-tvenvin kollu. Ħarset lil hinn, lejn waħx ta' infinità li ssoltu jserraħha. Illum imma xejn. Moħħha kien x'imkien ieħor.

Imbagħad tħares lejn il-mowbajl, tara l-ħin, tieħu żewġ nifsijiet twal, tiftaħ il-bieba tal-karozza u toħroġ 'il barra, tiġġieled mar-riħ biex tasal sat-tarf.

Tħares 'il quddiem lejn il-baħar bla tarf; u bejn tvenvina u oħra tgħajjat, "daqshekk!"

ONE DAY I'LL FLY AWAY

LARA CALLEJA

The winds were force six. Gusts threatened to pluck trees from their trunks and release them to god-knows-where. Car wheels levitated over the road, weightless, pleading to plummet down the precipice. The sky was clear. Exciting for those who don't have the guts. She punched the clutch and let it go; what if the hand break was not enough to keep the car anchored in the car park? Into the distance, she looked towards an infinite skyline that usually soothed her. But today, nothing. Her mind was elsewhere.

A glance at her phone, she checks the time, takes two long breaths, opens the car door, and fights the wind through the soft silt.

Looking forward to the endless sea, between two waves she shouts, "That's it!"

Language says a lot about the social psyche, trends, and way of living. Even the tone and pitch of a specific language sets an aesthetic landscape for native speakers. Of course, we can understand each other through global languages and artistic expression, but being 100% true to the story also means using the language it is rooted in.

TO LIVE WITH HOPE

FIONA MALLIA

ENGLISH TRANSLATION OF "GĦEXET BIT-TAMA"

NO, IT CAN'T BE," she said to herself. "How could he leave me in this situation?" Anna threw the last flower on her husband's coffin - the same husband, who until recently was still working in the quarries all day; from the time the sun rises until it gives its last kiss to the lazy sea, whose mind was only playing with the rocks worn by time. She was reminded of her husband's strong body lifting the heavy loads in the quarry, she saw him lift the children and play with them, she saw him take on the responsibility of a family that he cherished so much, and above all, she saw him surrounded by her in a moment of love.

The last prayer was said and then the creaking of the polished wood was heard, hitting the damp floors of the walls that were the refuge of those who were lucky enough to be thrown there. Now she definitely couldn't see him anymore ... now he was definitely cut from the list of the living ... now there was definitely no place left for him. The seal was given when the gravedigger, with a trowel in his hand, began to scrape the surface of that grave ... the grave that who knows when it would be opened again to welcome her within it?

These visions were lost in the air and in their place reality emerged - the cold and powerless body of this same man. With all these thoughts in her mind, she didn't even realize that the ceremony was over.

What was the consolation and condolence of the people worth? What was the embraces worth? Didn't she have to face life? How could she take care of the children alone when she usually always depended on this man? How could she live without him? "I have to see what needs to be done. I can't just sit around and mourn myself. Life must go on - both for me and for my children." The terrified words that came out of her mouth were lost in nothing because in her mind there was only him and only him.

At home, there was barely communication. In these last days, Anna had lost all interest in the children and she spent the days thinking... thinking about the loss of her husband, thinking about the situation she was in, thinking about the future. The future is like a stone that keeps rolling until it hits the cliff. But who knows if this stone should have found some protection and not continue to roll? Or who knows if you will find someone who will give it a kick and it will end prematurely?

Work opportunities were rather restricted for her since she barely had any educational qualifications. Most probably, she had would be faced with a job of too much suffering that no one would want to do and with low pay. Then, to feed two children with her!

She had left the children out of her life, even though she loved them. But she too immersed in her thoughts and sufferrings. How will she tell them about the situation? They are still young to understand. She had no one to leave them with, who could take good care of them. Lost in these thoughts, Anna did not even realize that Maria, her elder daughter of nine years, was observing every movement that her mother was doing.

"Mum", she said, trying to climb into her mother's lap, "when is dad coming? It isn't usual for him to take so long when he travels?"

"Daddy is not coming, beautiful", answered her mother promptly.

But the girl could not get this phrase down and without loss of time she grabbed her mother's hand and said in awe, "How come he is not coming? Dad loves us very much and he will definitely not leave us alone."

"Dad has traveled, Maria. He traveled and went to Heaven because God called him"

"So why didn't he call us all. We are all good and God loves us for sure," answered Maria in an innocent tone.

"Why don't you go and play with your brother? You know we're not supposed to leave him alone," Anna cut short.

"Sure, mum, I will." Maria left her mother and went to her brother without getting the desired answer.

Those words were enough for her to burst into tears. The tears rolled down her cheeks and as she looked at the window, she saw the raindrops sliding along the window pane. The air also seemed to be sad and the thunder had not stopped since morning. The aweful weather complimented the atmosphere inside the house. But the storm outside was to pass within two days. The storm inside Anna's heart did not know how long it would last. It could not last or else it could last until her name also was to be erased from the list of the living.

That evening, Anna plucked up courage and managed to spend it with the children. She had lost all interest in them. Without wanting to, the loss of her husband felt too much - his loss was bringing her closer to him - to death. But today she wanted to spend some time with them. She imagined them two little angels who should not be left to be carried away by this storm that who knows when it will last.

The younger child, Mario, had just turned six. He was a handsome young boy despite the disability he had from birth. His life was doomed to a wheelchair. Mario's innocent face would make you fall in love with him. Could that be that this boy was the key to the bitterness in her life? She did not know of any relatives who had the same problem. Or maybe because of the trouble she had in pregnancy because her sister was divorcing at that time? So did it have to affect that much? There was nothing to do. She loved the children equally.

"Be blessed my children," she told them with sadness in her heart, while she arranged the pillows under their heads and covered them with warm blankets. The children were happy that they still had their mother. Once there was someone who still loved and cared for them, they didn't really miss their father. Maybe because they were still young or maybe because they didn't spend much time with him. Who knows?

It was decided. She couldn't go on like this. She took a paper from the desk drawer and in a few words but clearly wrote:

Sister, I will leave you the most precious thing I have left - my children. Take care of them and look after their needs. As soon as I find a good job and earn quite a bit of money, I promise you that I'll come and pay you back for what you do with them.

Always yours,

your sister, Anna.

She still did not have her mind at rest because her sister was not very responsible. However, she had no one to leave them with and could not continue to take care of them without having a proper wage.

Her sister had married some seven years before, after she had spent her youth in idleness and laziness. Her marriage was a failure because she hadn't even reached a year, that she wasn't bored of married life. Entertainment was more to her liking and marriage was like a chain to her; that the more time began to pass, the more she began to feel it tightening around her neck and suffocating her. She didn't have children and thus wanted to return to living life as a single - without anyone commanding her.

"Who knows," Anna whispered to herself, "Will my children be a hindrance to her? I hope that she doesn't deny this proposal." She asked God to keep his hand on them and that she won't be back for long so she can take care of her beloved children. After all, Anna didn't want to throw them into an orphanage.

From a drawer in the cupboard she brought a large luggage, and put some things she might need in it. She did not forget to carry with her a recent photo of the entire family. She stopped looking at the mirror she had on the table in front of her. The reflection that appeared was nothing like the one Anna had seen a few months earlier. The happy and laughing eyes disappeared and the look in her eyes was dull and dark. The happy face turned into a sad and wrinkled one. The sad months that had passed over her were as if some fifty years had passed. She was bringing death closer, with her own hands. Life had to go on: both for the hardworking people who work tirelessly from dawn to dusk, for those who are lazy, for those who spend the day gossiping on others, and also for those who are sick and sad. Life makes us cry, makes us laugh, makes us show our feelings, but above all, hurts us.

She wiped the tears from her cheeks, picked up her clothes and left. She took one last glance at the house. Who knows how many special moments took place in that house? Who knows if the walls will remember what happened in that house? She was going to leave a treasure full of memories behind her that who knows when she will be lucky enough to reopen and continue to build on them. Who knows when she would live happily with her children again? Who knows how old they will be? Who knows if they will continue to love her because she will leave them? "But they are still too young for me to explain to them. They definitely don't understand me." She continued walking towards the neck of the road and posted the letter to her sister who lived at the edge of the village. She took a path that even she didn't know why she went through it. Who knows what will become of her?

*

Always yours,

your sister, Anna.

Doris' voice spelled out every word that was written on a piece of paper that her sister had left in the letter box the night before, and that because it was raining, it had become soiled. Although the words began to lose their shape, Doris still managed to read the message. It was all clear before her. Her sister left home because she could not raise a family.

"Blessed am I that I broke the bonds I had and that I did not have children." See what trouble my sister is in now? First she married and had two children, then life began to show her its majestic jaws with all cavities. The child came out not walking, then the death of her husband, who I don't know how she had continued to love him, and now - now she is desperate and has left the house to see what she will do to solve the problems she got into. Not only that, now she wanted to bother others. She will burden me with the weight of her children. Shall I go in for all this responsibility? I didn't even want to have children of my own and I'm going to worry about someone else's? But wait a minute, my sister has always been good to me. I never know that I lacked anything. Why shouldn't I help her? Who knows, maybe it won't be long before she comes back. She didn't even tell me where she was going. In short, there is nothing to do, I accept. Maybe it won't be long before she comes back.

Doris' anger turned into a series of thoughts that didn't stop ticking through the veins of her head. She wanted to scream and curse her luck. The release of her life was locked in a binding room - the binding of her sister's children. Who knows when she will be able to find the key and be able to open this door?

This novella is part of a long story. It deals with how the life of a wife-mother, Anna, changed overnight with the death of her husband on whom she depended so much. Lack of work and lack of money forced her to do what she didn't want to do. The decision she had to make was not going to affect just one person...

MEET THE AUTHORS & ARTISTS

OF THE FEMININE VOICE OF MALTA: IL-LEĦEN FEMMINILI TA' MALTA

MARIA GRECH GANADO

...has won National Book Prizes for 4 of her 8 poetry collections in Maltese or English and been translated into 12 other languages. In 2005 she co-organised an international seminar (RE-VISIONS) with LAF and Inizjamed in Malta. She has been awarded by the State, the University of Malta and her hometown, Floriana. Maria has 3 children and 3 grandchildren.

ANNA MARIA SCHURMANN

...was born in Malta and left in 2008 to serve as Malta's Consul General in New South Wales. She then served as the Palestine desk within the European External Action Service in Brussels, Belgium. In 2014, Anna Maria moved to Melbourne, Australia where she now lives with her husband Mark and their two daughters. Anna Maria has always had a love for reading, writing and sharing her stories of being born in a large close-knit family and then travelling and making friends around the world.

MIRIAM CALLEJA

...is a Maltese bilingual freelance poet, author, ghostwriter, workshop leader, and translator. She is the author of 3 poetry collections, 2 chapbooks, and several collaborative works. Her poetry are published in anthologies and in translation worldwide. Her latest title is *Come Closer, I Don't Mind the Silence* (BottleCap Press, 2023). Her essays and poems have appeared in platform review, *Odyssey, Whale Road Review, Tupelo Quarterly, Modern Poetry in Translation*, and elsewhere. Miriam is highly commended by the Stephen Spender Trust for her work in translation. She is currently working on a series of nonfiction hybrid essays.

KRISTINA BORG

...is a socially engaged artist and an art educator. In her transdisciplinary context-specific research-practice her work dialogues with multispecies communities and specific places, focusing on the co-creation of experiential, participatory and collaborative community projects. It relates to socio-political, economic, environmental and feminist issues in urban-collective spaces. She is a fellow of the *Salzburg Global Forum for Cultural Innovators* and the *International Community Economies Research Network*.

ELIZABETH GRECH

....works for Mana Chuma Teatro, where she is in charge of translation, communications and international relations. As a translator, she works with various cultural and artistic entities. She has translated several contemporary Maltese poets and writers into French. Her own poetry in the Maltese language has been published in anthologies and journals in several languages (French, Albanian, Mandarin). Her first poetry collection *bejn baħar u baħar* was published by Merlin Publishers in Malta (2019) and was later translated and published into Italian, Greek, Spanish, Arabic and English.

LARA CALLEJA

...published *Lucy Min?* and in 2020, *Kissirtu Kullimkien*. She won the European Literature Prize and two National Book Council awards. An activist for 18 years, Lara advocates against censorship, corruption, and environmental destruction, and also advocates for universal dignity. Her writing questions and challenges societal norms, exploring profound narratives through seemingly mundane stories. Additionally, in 2020, she ventured into theatre, marking her third theatrical playwright till present.

ANNA GRIMA

...born 1958, Malta, is an artist whose works have been exhibited in several European countries. Some of her work is held permanently in the National Art Collection of Malta through the Fondazzjoni Kreattività Art Collection.

RAMONA DEPARES

...is an award-winning journalist and author. For decades she was part of Times of Malta newsroom - during her tenure she received two journalism awards by the Istitut tal-Ġurnalisti Maltin, one for cultural journalism and another for op-ed writing.

Ramona has published three books. The first one, *Beltin: Stejjer Minn Nies Minsija* is a collection of real life stories that document the dying community of Valletta. *The Patient in Hospital Zero* is a collection of short stories, while *Katya: Easy on the Tonic*, is the authorised biography one of Malta's first openly trans women. Ramona runs her own culture website, a non-monetized project supporting the cultural scene in Malta, as well as her own freelance content business.

NADIA MIFSUD

...moved to France in 1998. She currently lives in Lyon, where she writes, teaches and sometimes translates. To date, she has published three books of poetry, one chapbook, one novel and a collection of short stories. Mifsud's poems have been awarded various prizes in Malta, including the National Book Prize twice: *kantuniera 'l bogħod* (Edizzjoni Skarta) (2016) and for V*arjazzjonijiet tas-Skiet* (2022). In 2022 she became Malta's third Poet Laureate.

VERONIKA MERCIECA

...is an interdisciplinary artist, writer, and soon-to-be maritime historian. Her past roles have included working as a curator and installation artist at the London Artooms fair, illustrating and creating comic books for various European projects, and serving on the jury for the Giornate Degli Autori Film Festival in Venice. While she prefers collaborative artistic projects, her writing has a more personal focus, exploring intimate, everyday observations, contradictions, and experiences. This personal approach is evident in her contributions, which were first published on her blog, *For the Chronicler*, and which are set in Malta and its sister island Gozo.

LEANNE ELLUL

...writes poetry and prose, and has published works for both adults and children mainly in Maltese but also in English. She was named Best Emerging Author in the 2016 National Book Prize, and her works for children have garnered various awards. Ellul won first place in the national competition for theatre writing in 2013, and the Novel for Youths Prize 2014 and 2023. Ellul lectures in Maltese language and literature and is active in NGOs organising a number of festivals and open mics, namely Inizjamed and HELA Foundation.

CLARE AZZOPARDI

... lives between two places — Malta and the Netherlands. She spends most of her time writing for children and adults. She taught Maltese literature for 24 years and was also head of the Maltese Department at the University of Malta Junior College. She has won many awards, and her novel *Castillo* and short story collection *Kulħadd ħalla isem warajh* were translated into different languages such as English, Arabic, and Italian.

FIONA MALLIA

...was born on June 6, 1979. She lives in Attard, which is a village in Malta. She received her education from state schools and graduated as a Maltese teacher from the University of Malta. She works as a Maltese teacher at De La Salle College. The Maltese language is very close to her heart and when inspired, she scribbles whatever comes to her mind on paper. She is interested in all kinds of writing. In 2012 she published an informative book on Maltese Culture, called *Il-Kultura Maltija* and is currently publishing a book aimed at children.

LORANNE VELLA

...is a Maltese writer, translator and performer based in Brussels. She has won the Malta National Book Council's National Book Prize several times, including Best Novel in Maltese or English for *Rokit* and *Marta Marta*. She is co-editor of the Maltese-language literary journal.

LOUIS BRIFFA

...was born in Attard in 1971. He is a Director within the Maltese Government. Briffa published three books of poems: *Bil-Varloppa* (2006), *The Tale of a Grasshopper and a Tomato and other Poems* (2009) and *Bil-Boqxiex* (2018). He won the National Poetry Prize in 2006. In 2020 he was awarded a *'Ġieħ Ħal Lija'* for his literary contribution. In 2007 the poet had a son, Bertrand.

CLAUDIA GUACI

...teaches Maltese literature at the Junior College and she is also a translator. In 2022 she published her second collection of poems called *Max-Xatt tat-Tamarisk* published by Kotba Calleja. She translated various childrens' books into Maltese for Merlin Publishers, among which, *Magni taż-Żmien* that won the National Book Prize in 2019. She is an active member of the NGO Inizjamed.

VERONICA VEEN

...is a cultural anthropologist and an art historian/archaeologists, specialized in symbolic anthropology and women's studies. She is active in the Maltese field since 1986. Malta and especially Gozo she considers her 'motherland'. Next to on the intriguing *Maltese Neolithic*, she wrote several books on women's history and life, among which: *Female Images of Malta; Goddess, Giantess, Farmeress* (1994), *The Maltese Cinderella and the Women's Storytelling Tradition* (2017), and *Lucija tells... Women's History and Experience of Life in Gozo, Malta* (2020).

BRENDA PRATO

....is a thirty-one-year-old woman. She is married to an Italian husband and she is a mother of a two-year old boy. She is a Catholic canon lawyer by profession and she obtained her licentiate from KU Leuven. She holds a Bachelor in Theology from the University of Malta and a Postgraduate Diploma in Matrimonial Canon Law and Jurisprudence. She is a scientific researcher with the Faculty of Theology & Religious Studies within KU Leuven. As of September 2024, she will also join the Faculty of Canon Law of KU Leuven once again to embark on her doctoral studies in canon law. Some of her hobbies include painting, hand-knitting and writing short stories and poems in Maltese.

AARON AQUILINA

...is an academic with the University of Malta's English Department. He teaches, researches, and publishes work around literary studies and continental philosophy, with a particular focus on feminism, queer theory, and death. His latest publication was the monograph *The Ontology of Death* (Bloomsbury, 2023). Aquilina is also a creative practitioner and writes poetry and short prose, with his latest published poem appearing in *Modern Poetry in Translation* (2023).

RITA SALIBA

... is an author of both prose and poetry. She took part in the 2016 edition of the Mediterranean Literature Festival, has won the Writing Contest for the Young three times, and translated two novels from Italian for Maltese. Rita is an author of novels for adults as well as collections of short stories and microstories.

LISA ZAMMIT

... is a poet (on particularly contemplative days), a graphic-designer and editor currently living in Glasgow. She graduated from the University of Malta with a B.A. in English and later completed an MLitt in Publishing from the University of Stirling, eager to pursue a creative career in publishing. She believes poetry is one of the most liberating mediums to express one's self, and aims to publish her poetry in the near-future. Although her work tends to revolve around heavier themes like trauma and politics, she tries to embrace new forms of writing. When she's not working on books, she's drawing funky digital characters to unwind from her day.

JAHEL AZZOPARDI

...is a freelance photographer and is currently working in the field of events and decorations. The passion to meet with different clients and provide an experience as well as great imagery has stemmed from this very project where it took a personal turn. Being able to make someone feel good as well as look good in their imagery is something that Jahel strives to work for.

International Human Rights Art Movement

The International Human Rights Art Movement (IHRAM) offers creative programs promoting freedom of expression, human rights, and social justice around the world. We envision a world where artist activism is honored as a human right, and a source of social change.

Visit *humanrightsartmovement.org* to see this change in action and browse our collection of groundbreaking anthologies, writing, fellowships and other programming.

Thank you for being part of a greater cause

Printed in France by Amazon
Brétigny-sur-Orge, FR